QUESTIONS THAT NEED TO BE ANSWERED

By
V. Glenn McCoy

Author of
RETURN TO THE OLD PATHS

QUESTIONS THAT NEED TO BE ANSWERED
By
V. Glenn McCoy

Copyright © 2022 World Video Bible School®
ISBN: 9780997753127

Originally published in 2011
by McCoy Publications

WVBS® is thankful to the V. Glenn McCoy family
for the right to republish this book for the Lord's Church.

All Scripture quotations are from
The New King James Version of the Bible,
unless otherwise specified. Copyright 1982, Thomas Nelson, Inc.

Printed in the United States of America
All Rights Reserved.

Published by
World Video Bible School®
25 Lantana Lane
Maxwell, Texas 78656
www.WVBS.org

TABLE OF CONTENTS

Introduction 1
1. What Must I Do to Be Saved? 3
2. Questions You Have Asked about the Church of Christ 23
3. Can One Be Saved by Faith Alone? 43
4. What Is Our Authority in Religion? 57
5. Why Be Baptized? 73
6. What Is The "One Baptism"? 83
7. Is the Bible from God or Man? 91
8. Why Should I Believe in Jesus As the Son of God? 105
9. Why Should I Believe in God? 121
10. Why Doesn't the Church of Christ
     Use Instrumental Music in Worship? 143
11. What Is the Role of Women in the Church? 159
12. The "Gift" of Tongues: Ecstatic Utterances
     or Actual Languages? 175
13. Why Elders in the Church? 195
14. Is Church Attendance Necessary? 217
15. The Lord's Supper: When Should We Observe It? 225
16. What about the Lord's Supper
     and the One-Cup Issue? 231
17. When Is the Second Coming of Christ? 243
18. What Is the "Rapture?" 261
19. How Can I Share the Message of Christ with Others? ... 273

INTRODUCTION

Quite often we are challenged to answer questions of spiritual importance when there is little time to research the subject. Even if we have the time, we may not know where to look for the answers. This author felt there was a need to have some of the most often asked questions answered in a single volume. Obviously, these answers are not intended to be exhaustive, but they are intended to give a brief response that may trigger deeper study.

CHAPTER 1
WHAT MUST I DO TO BE SAVED?

There is no more important question in all the world than this one. Every other question fades in importance when one considers that the eternal destiny of a soul is at stake.

Who Can Be Saved?

Salvation is only promised to those who believe, accept, and obey Jesus Christ. Peter declared about Jesus, *"Nor is there salvation in any other, for there is no other name under heaven given among men by which we must be saved."* (Acts 4:12 NKJV). Jesus stated, *"For if you do not believe that I am He, you will die in your sins."* (John 8:24). Also, He said *"Not every one who says to me, 'Lord, Lord,' shall enter the kingdom of heaven, but he who does the will of My Father, in heaven"* (Matt. 7:21).

Regardless of how honest and sincere a person may be, he must not accept a plan of salvation that has originated in the mind of man. Devising a plan of salvation to save sinful mankind is a function that belongs only to the Lord. If one wants to know what to do to be saved, he must listen to the Lord who has revealed His plan in the New Testament.

The Lord Wants All to Be Saved

God loved man and desired his salvation so much that He allowed His only begotten Son to die on a cross on behalf of mankind (John 3:16). Jesus desired man's salvation so much that He endured the agony of that Cross to make it possible for any obedient person to be saved (Heb. 12:2). Jesus died, was buried, and then was resurrected from the dead (I Cor. 15:3-4). Before returning to heaven Jesus gave the apostles the message that they were to preach in order for people to be saved. We usually refer to this charge as the Great Commission. It is recorded in three places in the New Testament.

The Great Commission

"Go therefore and make disciples of all the nations, baptizing them in the name of the Father and of the Son and of the Holy Spirit, teaching them to observe all things that I commanded you; and lo, I am with you always, even to the end of the age" (Matt. 28:19-20).

"And He said to them, 'Go into all the world and preach the gospel to every creature. He who believes and is baptized will be saved; but he who does not believe will be condemned'" (Mark 16:15-16).

"Then He said to them, 'Thus it is written and thus it was necessary for the Christ to suffer and rise from the dead the third day, and that repentance and remission of sins should be preached in His name to all nations, beginning at Jerusalem.'" (Luke 24:46-47).

Faithful to Their Commission

The apostles were faithful to the orders given by Jesus. Not many days after the Lord gave the Great Commission, the apostles began preaching that gospel message in Jerusalem, just as Jesus had instructed. Peter stood up with the eleven and told the people assembled on the day of Pentecost what they had to do to be saved. Three thousand of them believed the message they heard, repented of their sins, and were baptized into Christ (Acts 2:37-38). When one is saved he becomes a Christian and the Lord adds him to the church (Acts 2:47). He does not first do one thing to be saved from his sins, and then later do something else in order to be added to the church.

Today, if one desires to be saved, become a Christian, and be added to the Lord's church, he can do so by obeying the Lord, even as the people of the first century did. The plan of salvation remains the same as it has always been. What it did in the first century it will do in the 21st century.

The Lord has given several examples to us to show how we can become Christians. Please consider these:

THE CONVERSION OF THE THREE THOUSAND
(Acts 2:22-41)

A very large crowd of people was assembled on the day of Pentecost in Jerusalem. They heard Peter preach the gospel. They heard him accuse them of crucifying the very Son of God. They were pierced in their hearts and asked the question *"Men and brethren, what shall we do?"* (v. 37). It was in answer to this question that the people were told *"Repent, and let every one of you be baptized in the name of Jesus Christ for the remission of sins"* (v. 38).

We Must Give the Same Answer

When one desires to know what to do to be saved today, can we give any other answer than that which was given by Peter and the other apostles on the day of Pentecost? Of course, we cannot! Unfortunately, people who are given that same answer today do not always react in a favorable way as so many in that great audience did. They desired salvation, and when they were told what to do in order to obtain it, they responded as all sincere people should. *"Then, those who gladly received his word were baptized; and there were added that day about three thousand souls"* (v. 41).

Their Faith Was Obedient

From the reaction of the three thousand to the message preached, they obviously believed in Jesus. They were *"pierced to the heart"* (v. 37). They *"received his word"* (v. 41). However, faith without obedience was not enough for them to be saved. It yet remained for them to *"repent and be baptized"* in order for their sins to be removed (v.38). These instructions were so simple that the people could not misunderstand. They gladly obeyed and were saved, and the Lord added them to the church (v. 47).

The Message Hasn't Changed

The soul saving message that the three thousand heard is still the same message of salvation that must be preached and accepted today. When one responds to that message as the three thousand did, the result will be the same, the forgiveness of sins.

If those people had refused to obey that simple plan of salvation, they would have remained in a lost condition. The same must be true today for those who refuse to obey the same plan of salvation that was presented in the first century.

THE CONVERSION OF THE SAMARITANS
(Acts 8:5-12)

Philip went down to the city of Samaria and preached Christ to the people (v. 5). *"But when they believed Philip preaching the good news about the kingdom of God and the name of Jesus Christ, they were being baptized, men and women alike"* (v. 12).

The Samaritans **heard** the gospel. They **believed** in Jesus and were **baptized**. The Samaritans received the same plan of salvation that the three thousand did on the day of Pentecost. The result was the same. Those who responded in trusting, obedient faith were saved and became Christians.

When Christ is preached fully to a lost people, baptism will always be included in that message. To be true to the Word, the purpose of that baptism must always be the same as that which was clearly taught by Peter in Acts 2:38, *"Repent, and let each of you be baptized in the name of Jesus Christ for the forgiveness of your sins."*

THE CONVERSION OF THE ETHIOPIAN
(Acts 8:26-40)

"Then Philip opened his mouth, and beginning at this Scripture, he preached Jesus to him. Now as they went down the road, they came to some water. And the eunuch said, 'See, here is water. What hinders me from being baptized?' Then Philip said, 'If you believe with all your heart, you may,' And

he answered and said, 'I believe that Jesus Christ is the Son of God.' And he commanded the chariot to stand still. And both Philip and the eunuch went down into the water, and he baptized him. Now when they came up out of the water, the Spirit of the Lord caught Philip away; so that the eunuch saw him no more; and he went on his way rejoicing" (Acts 8:35-39 NKJV).

From this New Testament example of conversion we can learn four very important facts:

(1) Preaching "Jesus" Included Baptism

It should be observed that Philip *"Preached Jesus to him"* (v. 35). In preaching *"Jesus"* to this lost individual, Philip taught him what he must do in order to receive Jesus. Included in preaching *"Jesus"* was the necessity of baptism. When they arrived at a place where there was water the eunuch saw his opportunity to obey the Lord and have his sins forgiven.

(2) Baptism Is Not Sprinkling

We note that this was not a sprinkling or pouring of water, for both Philip and the eunuch went down into the water. There is neither command nor example for sprinkling in all of the New Testament. Baptism of the New Testament was always a burial, an immersion (Romans 6:3-4).

(3) Just Being Religious Is Not Enough

The eunuch was a religious man, but he was still not saved. He had traveled all the way from Ethiopia to Jerusalem in order to worship under the Law of Moses. While he was traveling home he was reading from the Old Testament Scriptures. He came upon a prophecy about Jesus (Isa. 53). However, he did not know Jesus or what Jesus required of him. He asked Philip to help him understand. It was not enough for the eunuch to be a religious man. In addition to being religious he needed to be obedient (Matt. 7:21).

(4) Confession of Jesus Is Necessary

The eunuch asked Philip about Jesus, and Philip seized this opportunity to tell the eunuch not only about the person of Jesus, but also what Jesus required of him to be saved. When the eunuch saw the water he asked Philip the question *"What hinders me from being baptized?"* (v. 36). The only thing that now remained between him and baptism for the remission of his sins was his confession of faith. When Philip told him this, he responded by saying, *"I believe that Jesus Christ is the Son of God"* (v. 37).

Having made that confession of faith, the eunuch was ready for baptism. Both Philip and the eunuch went down into the water and Philip immersed him for the remission of his sins. Could the Scriptures be more simple in describing what one must do in order to become a Christian? What did the eunuch do in order to have his sins forgiven and to become a member of the Lord's church? He *heard* the gospel (Acts 8:35-39). He *believed* in Jesus (v. 37). He *confessed* his faith (v. 37). He was *baptized* (v. 38).

In the case of the conversion of the three thousand, recorded in the second chapter of Acts, they were told to repent. Even though repentance is not specifically mentioned in the conversion of the eunuch, this does not suggest that he refused to repent. Repentance was as necessary for him as it was for the three thousand. As we study the Book of Acts, we notice that Luke does not always record all the requirements of salvation in each conversion, although they may be clearly implied.

However, it is interesting to note that in every case of conversion, baptism is specifically mentioned as a requirement for those who would be saved. We can rest assured that what was required of one to be saved was also certainly required of the others, for God is no respecter of persons (Acts 10:34).

THE CONVERSION OF CORNELIUS
(Acts 10:34-48, 11:14)

"And He ordered us to preach to the people, and solemnly to testify that this is the One who has been appointed by God as Judge of the living and the dead. Of Him all the prophets bear witness that through His name every one who believes in Him has received forgiveness of sins. While Peter was still speaking these words, the Holy Spirit fell upon all those who were listening to the message" (Acts 10:42-44). *"Surely no one can refuse the water for these to be baptized who have received the Holy Spirit just as we did, can he? And he ordered them to be baptized in the name of Jesus Christ"* (Acts 10:47-48).

The conversion of Cornelius and his household is the first record of Gentiles being accepted into Christianity. This was such an important occasion that the Lord sent down the Holy Spirit upon them even as he had done earlier to the Apostles. *"And as I began to speak, the Holy Spirit fell upon them, just as He did upon us at the beginning"* (Acts 11:15).

Not Saved by the Holy Spirit Falling on Them

The Holy Spirit falling on those who heard the Word did not save them. This was a sign to the Jews that the Gentiles were no longer to be treated as those not worthy to hear and obey the gospel. It was a sign to the Jews and Gentiles alike that the Gentiles from henceforth were to be accepted into the church (Acts 11:18, Acts 15:8).

Not Saved by Morality

If being good morally could save an individual, surely Cornelius would have been saved for he was an excellent man morally *"a devout man, and one who feared God with all his household, and gave many alms to the Jewish people, and prayed to God continually"* (Acts 10:2). Cornelius was a religious man and morally excellent, but he was not saved.

Ordered to Be Baptized

At the direction of the Lord, Peter went from Joppa to Caesarea to the home of Cornelius, who was a centurion, and there he preached to him as well as those who were with him. When Peter concluded the preaching *"He ordered them to be baptized in the name of Jesus Christ"* (Acts 10:48). When Cornelius and the others responded to the command of Peter, they were saved. *"And he shall speak words to you by which you will be saved, you and all your household"* (Acts 11:14). It was this same Peter who would years later write *"And corresponding to that, baptism now saves you"* (I Peter 3:21).

THE CONVERSION OF LYDIA
(Acts 16:13-15)

"And on the Sabbath day we went outside the gate to a riverside, where we were supposing that there would be a place of prayer; and we sat down and began speaking to the women who were assembled. And a certain woman named

Lydia, from the city of Thyatira, a seller of purple fabrics, a worshipper of God, was listening; and the Lord opened her heart to respond to the things spoken by Paul. And when she and her household had been baptized, she urged us saying, 'If you have judged me to be faithful to the Lord, come into my house and stay.' And she prevailed upon us" (Acts 16:13-15).

Lydia was a religious person, but she was religiously wrong. To her everlasting credit, when she learned that she was wrong, she did not hesitate to change religiously in order to be right. When she **heard** the gospel preached, she **believed** it and responded by being **baptized**, and was thereby saved by Jesus.

THE CONVERSION OF THE JAILER
(Acts 16:25-34)

"And after he brought them out, he said, 'Sirs, what must I do to be saved?' And they said, 'Believe in the Lord Jesus, and you shall be saved, you and your household.' And they spoke the word of the Lord to him together with all who were in his house. And he took them that very hour of the night and washed their wounds, and immediately he was baptized, he and all his household. And he brought them into his house and set food before them, and rejoiced greatly, having believed in God with his whole household" (Acts 16:30-34).

"What Must I Do?"

Before the jailer had the opportunity to hear the Word, he asked the question *"What must I do to be saved?"* (Acts 16:30) Paul and Silas told him *"Believe in the Lord Jesus, and you shall be saved"* (v. 31). Paul and Silas were about to introduce the jailer to the only One in all of the universe who could give him salvation.

First Needed to Believe in Jesus

At this point he did not believe in Jesus. Salvation always begins with believing. But, the jailer could not believe in Him until he was taught about Him (Romans 10:14). Telling him to believe in Jesus was not the end of the discussion, but rather, it was the beginning. Please notice *"And they spoke the word of the Lord to him together with all who were in his house"* (v. 32).

After Paul and Silas taught the jailer about Jesus, the jailer's baptism followed, *"and immediately he was baptized, he and all his household"* (v. 33).

More Than Belief Was Necessary

When the *"Word of the Lord"* was declared, the jailer believed. But, something in addition to believing in Jesus as God's Son was required of him. He was baptized. When the *"Word of the Lord"* was preached, it included baptism. The fact that he *"took them that very hour of the night and washed their wounds"* certainly indicates repentance on his part. Although the record does not specifically state that he repented, it certainly implies that he did.

Since his sins were washed away in baptism he had good reason to *"rejoice greatly"* (v. 34). To have his sins forgiven, as well as to become a Christian and to be added to the church, the jailer **heard** the gospel. He **believed** in Jesus. He **repented** of his sins. He was **baptized** into Christ (Romans 6:3-4). The plan of salvation is so very simple!

THE CONVERSION OF THE CORINTHIANS
(Acts 18:8)

"And Crispus, the leader of the synagogue, believed in the Lord with all of his household, and many of the Corinthians when they heard were believing and being baptized" (Acts 18:8).

Here we have a very brief account of the Corinthians being converted to Christ. They heard Paul preach the gospel. They believed and were baptized. What could be more simple?

THE CONVERSION OF THE EPHESIANS
(Acts 19:1-5)

When Paul went to Ephesus he found some who had been baptized under John's baptism. The baptism of John had not been valid since the time that the gospel was preached on the day of Pentecost in A.D. 33. Prior to that time people were baptized by John's baptism, looking forward to the coming of Christ. When Christ came and delivered the plan of salvation, it was for all men, for all time (Matthew 28:18-20).

Their Baptism Was Not Valid

Before these twelve men met Paul, they did not realize that their baptism was no longer valid. These disciples were religious and very sincere, but they stood in need of baptism into Christ. When Paul learned that they had been baptized into John's baptism he said, *"John baptized with the baptism of repentance, telling the people to believe in Him who was coming after him, that is Jesus"* (v. 5).

To the credit of the Ephesians they did not argue with Paul

that they were religious and should be left alone. What was their reaction? *"And when they heard this, they were baptized in the name of the Lord Jesus Christ"* (v. 5).

THE CONVERSION OF PAUL
(Acts 22:1-16, 9:1-18)

"And a certain Ananias, a man who was devout by the standard of the Law, and well spoken of by all the Jews who lived there, came to me, and standing near, said to me, 'Brother Saul, receive your sight!' And at that very time I looked up at him. And he said, 'The God of our fathers has appointed you to know His will, and to see the Righteous One, and to hear an utterance from His mouth. For you will be a witness for him to all men of what you have seen and heard. And now why do you delay? Arise and be baptized, and wash away your sins, calling on His name." (Acts 22:12-16).

Paul (Saul of Tarsus) had been a violent persecutor of Christians. When Christ appeared to him on the way to Damascus he was stricken blind. When Paul asked *"What shall I do, Lord?"* (v. 10), he was told by Jesus, *"Go on into Damascus; and there you will be told of all that has been appointed for you to do"* (v. 11).

Those with him took him into the city where he prayed and went without food or drink for three days. Most certainly, Paul was convinced that he had been wrong religiously. He realized that the One he had denied was truly God's Son.

"Why Do You Delay?"

You will notice that Jesus told Paul to go into Damascus and there he would be told what to do. In Damascus, he was told what to do by Ananias. He taught Paul about the Lord and concluded by saying, *"And now why do you delay? Arise and be baptized, and wash away your sins, calling on His name"* (Acts 22:16).

He **believed** in Jesus. He showed the fruits of **repentance** when he prayed and fasted for three days. He was then **baptized** (Acts 9:18). The purpose of that baptism was specifically stated by Ananias. It was to *"wash away your sins"* (v. 16).

Paul "Called Upon the Name of the Lord"

Romans 10:13 states that *"Whoever will call upon the name of the Lord will be saved."* In the example of the conversion of Paul we see exactly what is meant by that expression. When Paul obeyed the gospel and was baptized, he was *"calling on His name"* (v. 16).

If one wants to be saved today and have his sins washed away, then he should respond to the gospel in the same way as did Paul and the others whose conversions we have read about.

THE PLAN OF SALVATION

In the Book of Acts the Lord has given to us nine cases of New Testament conversions. From those examples one can clearly see what the Lord required of the people of the first century in order for them to be saved. If one seeks to become a child of God today, he can do no better than to study and follow those New Testament examples. If a sincere seeker of truth does today what those first century disciples did, the result will be the same. He will be saved and become a Christian. He will not be a member of any denomination, for the Lord will add him to His church. *"And the Lord added to the church daily those who were being saved"* (Acts 2:47 NKJV).

In addition to these examples, the Lord has given many other passages that also instruct us in this most important matter of becoming a child of God. No one need misunderstand what the Lord requires of us in order to be saved. **What is the plan of salvation?**

IN ORDER TO BE SAVED ONE MUST BELIEVE IN JESUS

Jesus said that we would die in our sins if we didn't believe in Him. *"For unless you believe that I am He, you shall die in your sins"* (John 8:24). He also said, *"He who has disbelieved shall be condemned"* (Mark 16:16).

In John 3:16 Jesus declared *"For God so loved the world, that He gave His only begotten Son, that whoever believes in Him should not perish, but have eternal life."*

This does not suggest that one is saved by believing only, for a few verses later Jesus elaborates on this by saying, *"But he who does not obey the Son shall not see life, but the wrath of God abides on him"* (John 3:36).

It is necessary to **believe** in Jesus. This is the beginning of the conversion process. Believing moves one in the direction of salvation (John 1:12). However, only believing or *"faith only"* will not save anyone.

IN ORDER TO BE SAVED ONE MUST REPENT OF SINS

Repentance is a change of mind that brings about a change of direction (Acts 26:20). The goodness of God leads one to repentance (Romans 2:4). God wants all to repent. *"The Lord is not slow about His promise, as some count slowness, but is patient toward you, not wishing for any to perish but for all to come to repentance"* (2 Peter 3:9).

We must **repent** so that our sins will be blotted out (Acts 3:19). Jesus made the necessity of repentance clear when he said *"I tell you, no, but unless you repent, you will all likewise perish"* (Luke 13:3).

Faith combined with **repentance** moves one in the direction of salvation.

IN ORDER TO BE SAVED
ONE MUST CONFESS FAITH IN JESUS

Making this good confession of faith leads one to salvation. *"For with the heart man believes, resulting in righteousness, and with the mouth he confesses, resulting in salvation"* (Romans 10:10).

Jesus promised a blessing to those who would confess Him and denial to those who denied Him. *"Every one therefore who shall confess Me before men, I will also confess him before My Father who is in heaven. But whoever shall deny Me before men, I will also deny him before My Father who is in heaven"* (Matthew 10:32-33). When the eunuch confessed Jesus he said, *"I believe that Jesus Christ is the Son of God"* (Acts 8:37).

Faith combined with **repentance** and **confession** of our faith in Jesus moves one in the direction of salvation.

IN ORDER TO BE SAVED
ONE MUST BE BAPTIZED

Jesus tied belief and baptism together as standing in front of salvation, *"He who has believed and has been baptized shall be saved, but he who has disbelieved shall be condemned"* (Mark 16:15-16). It wasn't necessary for Jesus to say, *"He who has disbelieved and is not baptized shall be condemned"* for unless one believes, he certainly would not be interested in baptism or any other act of obedience to the Lord. Salvation must begin with believing.

Jesus commanded baptism in Matthew 28:19: *"Go therefore and make disciples of all the nations, baptizing them in the name of the Father and the Son and the Holy Spirit."*

Peter preached that one not only repents but is baptized in order to receive the forgiveness of sins. *"Repent, and let each of you be baptized in the name of Jesus Christ for the forgiveness of your sins"* (Acts 2:38). That same Peter later declared *"Baptism now saves you."* (I Peter 3:21). Again, it was Peter who command Cornelius and his household to be baptized. *"And he ordered them to be baptized in the name of Jesus Christ"* (Acts 10:48).

In reading about New Testament conversions, one cannot help but be impressed with the urgency of baptism. In each case the person was baptized immediately: *"And he took them that very hour of the night and washed their wounds, and immediately he was baptized, he and all his household"* (Acts 16:33). There is no justification for waiting days, weeks, or even months to baptize one who has confessed his faith in Jesus. The urgency lies in the fact that forgiveness of sins does not take place until the candidate is baptized.

Those who would make baptism an unnecessary option need to carefully look at these passages. Baptism is not optional. It is essential if one is to be saved.

When one trusts in the Lord enough to obey Him by **believing** in Him, **repenting** of his sins, **confessing** Him, and being **baptized**, that person is saved. He is saved by the love, goodness, and grace of God!

SOME OBSERVATIONS:
About Sprinkling

If we learned about salvation simply from the New Testament teachings and examples and left out the innovations created by men, we would know nothing about sprinkling or pouring as a *"mode"* of baptism. There is only one baptism (Eph. 4:4). The form of the one baptism is a **burial** in water (Romans 6:3-4). Even the original Greek word for baptism (baptizo) meant to *"bury"* or *"dip"* or *"plunge."* Men introduced sprinkling without any authority from the Lord. Those who have been sprinkled have not been scripturally baptized.

About Infant Baptism

If we only took the New Testament as our authority, we would know nothing about infant baptism. New Testament baptism is for those who believe (Mark 16:16). Infants are not capable of believing. Baptism is for the remission of sins (Acts 2:38). Infants are not capable of sinning (Matthew 18:3). Infant baptism originated with men, not with the Lord.

About Being Voted into the Church

If we took only the New Testament as our source of information and authority, we would know nothing about voting someone into the church. When one is baptized into Christ (Galatians 3:26-27) he is added to the church by the Lord (Acts 2:47). Men have interposed their will in the matter of church membership. You can search the New Testament from cover to cover and you will not find anyone who was voted into the church.

About Being Saved

It is a wonderful thought to realize that any responsible person can become a child of God today. He can do so by accepting salvation on the simple terms that the Lord has set down.

In this booklet we have taken great care to present only those requirements for salvation that the Lord has set forth in his Word. We have refrained from including anything that man has devised, for man has no part in determining what is required in order to be saved.

You can become a Christian today just as those disciples of the first century did. In doing so, you will be saved from your sins, become a member of the Lord's church, and heaven itself will be set before you as your eternal destination.

CHAPTER 2
QUESTIONS YOU HAVE ASKED ABOUT THE CHURCH OF CHRIST

In thousands of communities in the United States and throughout the world you will find congregations of the church of Christ. If you have visited one of these congregations, you may have had questions about what you saw there and heard taught. In this chapter we would like to answer some of the questions that are often asked about the church. In doing so, we do not place ourselves in a position of authority, for such authority belongs only to the Lord.

We do not present this chapter as the creed for the church of Christ, for the New Testament is the only creed that we have. We rely solely on the Bible to know what pleases or displeases Him. Our answers must be based upon Biblical principles and teachings and not on positions taken by religious legislative bodies, conventions, councils, or synods.

"Is the Church of Christ a New Church?"

No, the church of Christ is not a new church. It was founded by Jesus in Jerusalem in the first century. This makes it hundreds of years older than any denomination in existence today. In Matt. 16:18 Jesus made this promise: *"I will build my church."* (NKJV). On the day of Pentecost in A.D. 33 that promise was fulfilled and the church of Christ came into existence. On that day the gospel was first preached by Peter and the other apostles. In doing so, the Lord's plan of salvation was revealed: *"Repent and let every one of you be baptized in the name of Jesus Christ for the remission of sins."* (Acts 2:38).

Those who responded had their sins forgiven and were added to the church of Christ (Acts 2:47). Members of the church of Christ today are members of that same church that was established over 1900 years ago.

"What Is the Distinctive Plea of the Church of Christ?"

Members of the church of Christ today want to restore the original New Testament church. To do this, it is necessary to set aside the creeds and doctrines created by men. We must go back beyond all the denominations that men have established, back to the pattern for that church left for us in the New Testament.

To be God's true people, we must take the Bible alone as the authority in all things religious. Therefore, we strive to give a *"thus saith the Lord"* for that which we teach and practice. We need to *"speak where the Bible speaks and remain silent where the Bible is silent."* If we teach the pure Word of God today, we are planting the same seed that was planted in the first century. When that seed was planted then, Christians and only Christians were produced and the church came into existence. The plea of members of the church of Christ today is for religious unity based upon the Word of God.

"Isn't the Church of Christ Just Another Denomination?"

No, the church of Christ is **not** a denomination, nor is it a part of a denomination. To suggest that the church of Christ is a denomination is to suggest that it is one of many, or a part of the whole, in the same way that a dollar bill is one denomination of the U.S. currency. The church that we read about in the New Testament could never be classified as such. When the church came into existence in A.D. 33, no one needed to ask the Christians to which denomination they belonged, for there was only one church. All who were members of the church were simply Christians.

We firmly believe that the same should be true today. The New Testament teaches *"There is one body"* (Eph. 4:4), and that the "body" is the church. *"And He is the head of the body, the church."* (Col. 1:18). Therefore, there is only one church. While many seem to glory in there being many denominations, the Lord prayed that all of his followers would be one. *"I do not pray for these alone, but also for those also who will believe in Me through their word; that they may all be one"* (John 17:20-21). The apostle Paul condemned division among Christians. *"Now I plead with you brethren, by the name of our Lord Jesus Christ, that you all speak the same thing, and that there be no divisions among you, but that you be perfectly joined together in the same mind and in the same judgment"* (Cor. 1:10).

The church of Christ is neither Protestant, Catholic, or Jewish, but simply the church that Jesus established, the one for which he died (Acts 20:28). Preaching the same gospel that was preached by the apostles and obeying the same conditions of salvation will reproduce the church of Christ in any period of time, in any place in the world.

"Who Is the Head of the Church of Christ?"

Unlike denominations, the church of Christ does not have an earthly head, nor does it have an earthly headquarters. It does not have a human creed. It does not have a universal organization. It does not have policy making conventions or even elected officers such as presidents and vice-presidents. No man on earth can rightfully claim to be head over the church of Christ. The only head of the church is Jesus: *"And He is the head of the body, the church; who is the beginning, the first born from the dead"* (Col. 1:18).

Jesus has all authority over the church, and he has never relinquished that power to anyone on earth. *"And Jesus came up and spoke to them, saying, 'All authority has been given to Me in heaven and on earth.'"* (Matt. 28:18). The headquarters for the church of Christ is in heaven.

"If There Is No Earthly Headquarters, How Is the Church Governed?"

Each congregation is self-ruling, or autonomous, being independent from every other congregation of the church. The only tie that binds the thousands of congregations together throughout the world is a common allegiance to the Lord and the Bible. No person or group of people can issue policies to other congregations or make decisions for them.

The church of Christ is governed by the authority of the Word of God. In each congregation, as men are recognized to possess the qualifications set down in the Scriptures (see I Tim. 3:1-12 and Titus 1:5-9), a plurality of men are selected to be elders. They are also called bishops. These men have the oversight **only** of the congregation over which they were appointed. Deacons, who are special servants, are also appointed in each congregation.

"Why Doesn't the Church of Christ Use Instruments in Their Worship?"

This is one of the most commonly asked questions about the church. There are fundamental reasons why we do not use pianos, organs, or other instruments of music in our worship.

Churches of Christ plead for a return to first century faith and practice. A careful study of New Testament teaching on the subject will reveal that there is no scriptural authority for using instruments in worship. Everything believed and practiced in religion must have divine authority behind it. *"And whatever you do in word or deed, do all in the name of the Lord Jesus, giving thanks to God the Father through Him"* (Col. 3:17). To do something in the name of the Lord is to do it by His authority.

Christians are to *"walk by faith, not by sight"* (2 Cor. 5:7). That faith comes only from the Word of God, *"So then faith comes by hearing, and hearing by the word of God"* (Rom. 10:17). The true disciple is concerned about those things that are specifically forbidden, as well as respecting the silence of the Scriptures. A respect for the silence of the Scriptures will keep us from adding things that are not authorized. In God's Word we read of the disastrous results of those who tried to offer unauthorized worship to God. (I Sam. 13:11-14, II Chron. 26, Lev. 10:1-17).

The church of the first century did not use instruments of music in their worship. In fact, it was several hundred years after Jesus established his church that the apostate church introduced instruments into their worship about AD 670. This caused such a furor that the instrument was speedily removed in order to avert a split. It was not introduced again until about AD 800. Since the New Testament leaves out the use of instrumental music in worship, we must leave it out.

The New Testament passages that deal with the subject of music in worship are Matt. 26:30, Mark 14:26, Acts 16:25, Rom. 15:9, I Cor. 14:15, Eph. 5:19, Col. 3:16, and Heb. 2:12. In **every** case the authorized music is singing. The Lord never authorized instrumental music in worship. No apostle ever sanctioned it. No New Testament writer ever commanded it or condoned it. No New Testament church ever practiced it. The practice of using instrumental music in worship was born in a church that hardly resembled the church that Jesus established. Instrumental music in worship today has no more sanction than the burning of incense or the offering of animal sacrifices.

"How Does One Become a Member of the Church of Christ?"

Since the church belongs to Jesus (Matt. 16:18), and He is its only head (Eph. 1:22), and all authority has been given to Him (Matt. 28:18), the terms of entrance must be determined by Him. The same obedience that makes one a Christian is also the basis on which the Lord adds one to the church. *"The Lord added to the church daily those who were being saved"* (Acts 2:47). *"He has delivered us from the power of darkness and conveyed us into the kingdom of the Son of His love"* (Col. 1:13).

Faith Is Required

Jesus said, *"For if you do not believe that I am He, you will die in your sins."* (John 8:24). He also said, *"But he who does not believe will be condemned."* (Mark 16:16). We must believe, for *"But without faith it is impossible to please Him"* (Heb. 11:6). Faith alone does not make one a Christian, but it is the first step toward being a child of God and becoming a member of His church, *"For with the heart one believes unto righteousness"* (Rom. 10:10).

Repentance Is Commanded

"Truly, these times of ignorance God overlooked, but now commands all men everywhere to repent" (Acts 17:30). Repentance is a turning away from sin in order to have that sin removed. *"Repent therefore and be converted, that your sins may be blotted out"* (Acts 3:19). God's desire is *"for all to come to repentance"* (2 Pet. 3:9).

Confession of Christ Is Necessary

The apostle Paul wrote that we are to confess with our mouth *"Jesus as Lord"* (Rom. 10:9). Jesus said, *"Every one therefore who shall confess Me before men, I will also confess him before My Father who is in heaven"* (Matt. 10:32). Before the Ethiopian eunuch could be baptized, it was necessary for him to confess *"I believe that Jesus Christ is the Son of God"* (Acts 8:37). This is the same good confession that one must make today prior to being baptized.

Baptism Is Necessary for One to Become a Christian and to Be Added to the Church

According to the Lord's statement in Mark 16:16, no one can be saved from his past sins until he has been baptized. *"He who has believed and is baptized will be saved"* (Mark 16:16). Jesus joined faith and baptism as conditions for salvation. One is just as necessary as the other.

Before Jesus returned to heaven, He gave His Great Commission to His apostles. He told them to go preach, and baptize those who believed for the remission of their sins (Matt. 28:18-20, Mark 16:15-16, Luke 24:46-47).

Peter was obeying the instructions of Jesus when he stood up on the day of Pentecost and declared, *"Repent and let every one of you be baptized in the name of Jesus Christ for the remission of sins"* (Acts 2:38). Those who responded to the preaching of Peter were baptized into Christ and received the forgiveness of their sins, and they were added to the church (Acts 2:47).

When Peter had the privilege of preaching the gospel to Gentiles, *"He commanded them to be baptized in the name of the Lord"* (Acts 10:48). This same Peter later wrote, *"There is also an antitype which now saves us – baptism (not the removal of the filth of the flesh, but the answer of a good conscience toward God."* (I Pet. 3:21). Saul of Tarsus was told, *"Arise, and be baptized, and wash away your sins, calling on His name"* (Acts 22:16). What was true in New Testament times is just as true today. If one desires to have the forgiveness of his sins, he must believe, repent of his sins, confess Jesus, and be baptized.

Paul taught that baptism puts one into Christ. *"Or do you not know that as many of us as were baptized into Christ Jesus were baptized into his death?"* (Rom. 6:3). We read a similar expression in Paul's letter to the Galatians: *"For as many of you who as were baptized into Christ have put on Christ"* (Gal. 3:27). The only way to get *"into Christ"* is to be baptized into Him. To be *"in Christ"* is to be in his body, and his body is the church (Eph. 1:22,23). "For by one Spirit we were all baptized into one body" (I Cor. 12:13).

The answer to the question *"How does one become a member of the church of Christ?"* is the same answer to the question, *"How does one become a Christian?"* When one responds to the grace of God and obeys the gospel, he is saved, and the Lord takes care of his membership in His church, for it is the Lord who adds him to his church, *"And the Lord added to the church daily those who were being saved"* (Acts 2:47). There is no *"agony of uncertainty,"* no filling out of applications, no experience to relate, and no voting anyone into the church.

"Why Do You Baptize by Immersion?"

Eph. 4:5 tells us that there is *"One Lord, one faith, one baptism."* It is quite easy to determine that the *"one baptism"* of the New Testament is immersion. The word *"baptize"* comes from the Greek *"baptizo"* which literally means *"to dip, to immerse, to plunge."* If we knew no more than the meaning of the word that was used to describe this act, it should be adequate to convince the honest truth seeker that there is not now, nor has there ever been, Biblical authority for sprinkling or pouring. The very word means burial.

As we look at the Scriptures pertaining to baptism, we can reach no other conclusion but that New Testament baptism was by immersion. *"Therefore we were buried with Him through baptism into death, in order that just as Christ was raised from the dead by the glory of the Father, even so we also should walk in newness of life"* (Rom. 6:4). When one is baptized scripturally he will be buried and raised up. This could only describe baptism by immersion.

"Buried with Him in baptism, in which you also were raised with Him through faith in the working of God, who raised Him from the dead" (Col. 2:12). Again, baptism is described as a burial and a raising up. There is no way that this description of baptism will fit sprinkling or pouring.

When we look at an example in the New Testament where one was actually baptized, we can see for certain that true baptism was a burial in water. *"So he commanded the chariot to stand still; and both Philip and the eunuch went down into the water, and he baptized him. And when they came up out of the water, the Spirit of the Lord caught Philip away; and the eunuch saw him no more, and he went on his way rejoicing"* (Acts 8:38-39). Baptism included both the preacher and the one being baptized going **down into** the water, and following the baptism, **coming up** out of the water.

The baptism of the Great Commission is the only baptism that is authorized today. However, in the religious world we see a number of baptisms being practiced. We can determine if a baptism is the true, scriptural one by comparing what we see practiced with that which is described in the Scriptures:

After the Great Commission Was Given, There Was Only One Valid Baptism (Eph. 4:4).

1. It was in water (Acts 8:37).
2. It was a burial in water (Rom. 6:4, Acts 8:35-39).
3. It was a resurrection from the water (Col. 2:12).
4. It was administered by men (Matt. 28:19).
5. It was for the people of the whole world (Mark 16:15).
6. It was to last until the end of time (Matt. 28:20).
7. It was administered in the name of the Father, Son, and Holy Spirit (Matt. 28:19).
8. It was for the purpose of obtaining the forgiveness of sins. (Acts 22:16, Acts 2:38).
9. It put one into Christ (Rom. 6:3, Gal. 3:27).
10. It was only for those who were capable of believing (Mark 16:16).

"Why Does the Church of Christ Place Such Emphasis on Baptism?"

Since the Bible is the divine Word of God, we must place the same emphasis on baptism that was placed on it by the Lord, no more and no less. And what emphasis did the Lord place on baptism? He said that no one could be saved from his past sins until he had been baptized. *"He who believes and is baptized will be saved"* (Mark 16:16). How can we refrain from emphasizing something that stands between one being saved or being lost eternally?

The Apostle Peter said that baptism results in the forgiveness of sins (Acts 2:38), and that baptism now saves us (I Pet. 3:21). Ananias told Saul that baptism washes away sin (Acts 22:16). We would be remiss if we failed to give baptism the same place in the plan of salvation as the Lord did.

The New Testament places baptism as standing between the sinner and soul saving relationships. Please give serious consideration to the vital role that baptism plays.

1. Baptism stands between the sinner and salvation (Mark 16:16).
2. Baptism stands between the sinner and the forgiveness of sins (Acts 2:38).
3. Baptism stands between the sinner and his sins being washed away (Acts 22:16).
4. Baptism stands between the sinner and his becoming a child of God (Gal. 3:26-27).
5. Baptism stands between the sinner and his getting into Christ (Rom. 6:3).
6. Baptism stands between the sinner and membership in the church (I Cor. 12:13).

"Why Does the Church of Christ Observe the Lord's Supper Every Sunday?"

We observe the Lord's Supper every Sunday because that is what the church of the first century did as they were led by the Apostles. We have their approved example to follow. Acts 20:7 contains a clear reference to the **weekly** observance of the Lord's Supper. *"Now on the first day of the week, when the disciples gathered together to break bread, Paul, ready to depart the next day, spoke to them and continued his message until midnight"* (NKJV). They did not meet yearly, quarterly, or even monthly to observe the Lord's Supper. They met weekly. This is an authoritative example for the church to follow as long as time will last.

The purpose of the weekly assembly of the church was to *"break bread,"* meaning to observe the Lord's Supper, to remember Jesus in the manner He had instructed. Jesus had commanded this observance in Matt. 26:26-28 and Luke 22:19. Paul mentions the same thing in I Cor. 11:24-25.

Concerning the assembly, the church had a direct command not to forsake it (Heb. 10:25). It was the practice of the first century Christians to meet for worship each week on the first day, Sunday. When they did so, they ate the Lord's Supper (I Cor. 11:20). The first day of the week is the Lord's Day. It was the day that Jesus arose from the grave. It was the day the church was established.

Someone might suggest that there is no indication in Acts 20:7 that the disciples came together every week. In the Old Testament the Jews received the Ten Commandments. The fourth commandment stated *"Remember the Sabbath day, to keep it holy"* (Ex. 20:8). Please notice that this verse does not say every Sabbath day, but it could mean nothing else. The Jews understood it to be every week. Each week included a seventh day or Sabbath, and every faithful Jew kept that day holy under the law of Moses.

Likewise, in the Christian dispensation, in the cycle of every seven days there comes a first day of the week. This is the *"Lord's Day"* and Christians are to *"break bread"* upon this day. The regularity of this observance should be no more a question for the Christian than the observance of the Sabbath was for the Jews under the Law of Moses.

In additional to internal proofs in the New Testament, respected historians have recorded that it was the practice of the Christians in those early centuries to meet and observe the Lord's Supper every Sunday.

"What Do Members of the Church of Christ Believe ...?"

While it is impossible to say what all members of the church of Christ believe on any given subject, there is general agreement by most members of the church of Christ on the subjects that will be discussed briefly in this section.

"What about the Trinity (Godhead)?"

We believe there is one God (I Tim. 2:5), but there are three persons in that one Godhead. *"For in Him dwells all the fullness of the Godhead bodily"* (Col. 2:9 NKJV). The three members of the Godhead are the Father, Son, and Holy Spirit. *"When he had been baptized, Jesus came up immediately from the water; and behold, the heavens were opened to him, and He saw the Spirit of God descending like a dove, and alighting upon Him; and suddenly a voice came from heaven, saying, 'This is My beloved Son, in whom I am well pleased'"* (Matt. 3:16-17). This passage makes reference to all three members of the Godhead.

"What about Verbal or Plenary Inspiration of the Bible?"

We believe in the verbal, plenary inspiration of the Bible. *"Knowing this first, that no prophecy of Scripture is of any private interpretation, for prophecy never came by the will of man, but holy of God spoke as they were moved by the Holy Spirit"* (2 Pet. 1:20-21).

More than 2,600 times the Bible lays claim to divine authorship for itself with such expressions as *"The Lord said,"* *"God spoke,"* *"The Word of Jehovah came to me saying."* The Lord revealed the contents of the Bible through the Spirit. *"But God has revealed them to us through His Spirit; for the Spirit searches all things, yes, the deep things of God ... these things we also speak, not in words which man's wisdom teaches but which the Holy Spirit teaches, comparing spiritual things with spiritual"* (I Cor. 2:10-13).

When we speak of the verbal or plenary inspiration, we mean total inspiration. We believe that the whole Bible is inspired. Paul told Timothy *"All Scripture is given by inspiration of God and is profitable for doctrine, for reproof, for correction, for instruction in righteousness; that the man of God may be complete, thoroughly equipped for every good work"* (2 Tim. 3:16-17). There is not a part of the **original** writings of the apostles and prophets which is not inspired. We are a people who believe in God's Book! Since it came from God it is **the** authority in all religious matters. If we can't justify a practice or a teaching from the Word, we have no business practicing it or teaching it.

"What about Spiritual Gifts?"

Special gifts were given to some Christians in the early days of the church. These included gifts such as healing, effecting of miracles, prophecy, and speaking in foreign languages they had never learned (I Cor. chapters 12 and 14). These were only temporary gifts to last until the New Testament was completed. Their purpose being served, they passed away. *"Love never fails; but whether there are prophecies, they will fail; whether there are tongues, they will cease; whether there is knowledge, it will vanish away. For we know in part, and we prophesy in part; but when that which is perfect has come, then that which is in part will be done away."* (I Cor. 13:8-10). The original purpose of special gifts has been served by the completed Word of God. Therefore, people do not posses these miraculous gifts today.

"What about Miracles in the Bible?"

The Bible records many miracles. We believe that every one of them happened exactly as they were recorded. In the New Testament, the purpose of the miracles was to authenticate that Jesus was from God. *"...Jesus the Nazarene, a Man attested by God to you by miracles, wonders, and signs which God through Him in your midst, as you yourselves also know"* (Acts 2:22). They were also to confirm that the message of the apostles and prophets came from God. *"And they went out and preached everywhere, the Lord working and confirming the word through the accompanying signs"* (Mark 16:20). The miracles, signs, and wonders did exactly as they were intended to do and then passed from the scene.

"What about the Resurrection of Jesus?"

The greatest miracle of the New Testament was the resurrection of Jesus. We confidently believe that Jesus rose from the dead on the Sunday morning following his death by crucifixion. After Jesus was buried, the Roman seal was set, the guards were posted. That was on Friday, but when they looked in the tomb on the third day, the body of Jesus was gone!

After He was seen dead, and was resurrected, He made at least 10 different appearances to men. He was seen alive by more than 500 people after he had been killed! In desperation, His enemies searched for his body or anything that they could use to counter the resurrection story. They could find nothing! No contradictory evidence was ever presented that Jesus did not rise from the dead. His disciples so believed in the resurrected Christ that they gave their very lives in preaching that message. We still preach the resurrected Christ!

"What about the Virgin Birth of Jesus?"

"Behold, the virgin shall be with child, and shall bear a Son, and they shall call his name Immanuel, which is translated, 'God with us'" (Matt. 1:23). We unashamedly believe and proclaim that Jesus was born of the virgin Mary. She was a virgin when she conceived Jesus, and she was still a virgin when she gave birth to Him. *"And kept her a virgin until she gave birth to a Son; and he called his name Jesus"* (Matt. 1:25). An all-powerful God who could create the heavens and the earth (Gen.1:1) could certainly bring His Son into this world in any manner that He chose, including being born of a virgin. If one is inclined to doubt the virgin

birth of Jesus, how can he consistently believe in the God who sent Him here? *"But when the fullness of the time came, God sent forth His Son, born of a woman, born under the Law"* (Gal. 4:4). We believe God. We believe the Bible. And, we believe in the virgin birth of Jesus.

"What about Miracles Today?"

We do not believe that authentic miracles are performed today. Sometimes we are told by so-called *"faith healers"* that a miracle has been performed, but never anything that can be proven or verified as a miracle. Also, many times things are called miracles that are simply the Lord working through natural means. Some call a recovery from a serious illness a miracle. A narrow escape from a tragedy is often called a miracle. The wonder of childbirth is called a miracle by some. While these are wonderful things, they are not miracles. For a true miracle to occur, a natural law must be suspended. We believe that today God works **through** natural laws rather than in **violation** of them.

Miracles were helpful during the infancy period of the church, before the written Word was completed. When Paul wrote to the Corinthians, he made it clear that the age of miracles was not to continue indefinitely. *"But when that which is perfect has come then that which is in part will be done away."* (I Cor. 13:10).

To deny that miracles are performed today does not mean that we deny the power of prayer. We believe in prayer, and we believe that God answers prayer. *"And whatever things you ask in prayer, believing, everything you ask in prayer, believing, you will receive"* (Matt. 21:22). Through prayer the sick are healed and blessings are showered upon us.

"What about Predestination?"

Paul said *"Just as He chose us in Him before the foundation of the world, that we should be holy and without blame before Him in love, having predestined us to adoption as sons by Jesus Christ to Himself, according to the good pleasure of His will"* (Eph. 1:4-5.) Paul was not talking about God pre-selecting individuals to be saved or lost, even against their own will. He was talking about a class of people, Christians, those who would choose Him, trust Him, and obey Him. These would be saved.

If the teachings of John Calvin were true, that is, that specific ones were pre-chosen to be saved and other specific individuals were pre-chosen to be lost, this would make God a respecter of persons. That cannot be. The Apostle said, *"In truth I perceive that God shows no partiality"* (Acts 10:34).

The New Testament speaks of the free will of man being able to respond to the Lord in order to be saved. *"Not everyone who says to me 'Lord, Lord,' shall enter the kingdom of heaven, but he who does the will of My Father in heaven"* (Matt. 7:21). *"For whoever calls on the name of the Lord shall be saved"* (Rom. 10:13). The Lord has given all of us the free will to choose or to reject Him. The reason that people are lost is because they make the wrong choice.

"What about Premillennialism?"

We do not believe the doctrine of premillennialism. This doctrine basically says that Christ will come again to the earth to establish an earthly kingdom in Jerusalem. This kingdom will supposedly last for 1,000 years and then the end will come. Indeed, Jesus is coming again, but He is not coming to establish His kingdom here on earth. That kingdom **came** in the first century. While Jesus was on earth He promised that the kingdom would be established **within the lifetime** of those listening to Him. *"And he said to them, 'Assuredly, I say to you that there are some standing here who will not taste death till they see the kingdom of God present with power'"* (Mark 9:1). If the kingdom has not yet come, some of the people who were listening to Jesus speak are now almost 2,000 years old!

In Matthew 16:18-19, when Jesus promised to build His church, He used the terms *"church"* and *"kingdom"* interchangeably. The church was established on the day of Pentecost, A.D. 33. From that time forth the kingdom, the church, is spoken of in the New Testament as being in existence. The Apostle Paul spoke of the kingdom as being in existence when he wrote the letter to the Colossians. *"He has delivered us from the power of darkness and conveyed us into the kingdom of His love"* (Col. 1:13).

Those who wait for an earthly kingdom should listen carefully to the words of Jesus as He described the nature of His kingdom. *"My kingdom is not of this world"* (John 18:36). We do not wait for that which is already here. As Christians, we are now citizens of that kingdom, members of that church.

When Jesus comes again, Christians who are alive will be *"caught up together with them in the clouds to meet the Lord in the air, and thus we shall always be with the Lord"* (I Thess. 4:17). The Scriptures do not tell us that Jesus will ever set foot on earth when He comes again, much less establish an earthly kingdom.

A Final Plea

The desire of churches of Christ today is to restore the model church of the first century. That restoration must include its organization, worship, and apostolic teaching. In the first century when the pure Word of God was planted in honest hearts, accepted and obeyed, Christians, and only Christians, were produced. When those New Testament Christians banded together, they became congregations of the church of Christ. Exactly the same thing will happen today.

We can restore the church that we read about in the New Testament. But, it will be necessary to discard the human creeds that blind us, and the man-made organizations that hinder us. We must put our trust solely in the Lord and His Word for the divine pattern of what He wants His church to be. The pattern is still there. It always has been. If we want to please the Lord, we will follow it.

CHAPTER 3
CAN ONE BE SAVED BY FAITH ALONE?

What Must I Do to Be Saved?

Quite often when people ask *"What must I do to be saved?"* they are told, *"All you have to do is believe and you will be saved."* Is this true? Is that what the Bible teaches? Are we really saved by faith alone? No, the Bible does not teach this popular doctrine. We are saved by faith, but not by faith alone. God requires more of us than simply believing in Jesus in order to be saved. Sadly, many trusting people are being given the wrong answer to the question about their salvation.

Teaching the doctrine of salvation by faith only will have disastrous consequences. If faith is the only condition of salvation, then there is nothing else the sinner needs to do in order to be pardoned. On the other hand, if there are other conditions that the Scriptures require, but one is convinced that faith only is enough, that individual will stop short of doing the will of the Lord, and will fall short of receiving the forgiveness of sins.

What Is Faith?

Hebrews 11:1 describes faith in this way, *"Now faith is the substance of things hoped for, the evidence of things not seen"* (NKJV). Faith is something not seen, but there is assurance involved in our faith. Faith must be based on testimony and evidence that results in certain convictions. Faith then expresses itself in definite actions in response to what the Lord has commanded.

Saved by...

The Bible says that we are saved by faith (John 3:16, Acts 16:31), but nowhere does it say that we are saved by faith **alone**. In addition to being saved by faith, the Scriptures speak of many things by which we are saved. Consider the following fifteen things by which the New Testament says that we are saved:

1. We are saved by the **WORD** (James 1:21).
2. We are saved by **PREACHING** (I Cor. 1:21).
3. We are saved by **REPENTANCE** (2 Cor. 7:10).
4. We are saved by **GOD** (I Timothy 2:3-4).
5. We are saved by **CONFESSION** (Romans 10:10).
6. We are saved by **JESUS** (Matthew 18:11).
7. We are saved by the **BLOOD of JESUS** (I Peter 1:18-19).
8. We are saved by the **GOSPEL** (Rom. 1:16).
9. We are saved by **OBEDIENCE** (Heb. 5:8-9).
10. We are saved by **GRACE** (Eph. 2:8-9).
11. We are saved by **BAPTISM** (I Pet. 3:21).
12. We are saved by **HOPE** (Rom. 8:24).
13. We are saved by **MERCY** (Titus 3:5).
14. We are saved by **WORKS** (James 2:24).
15. We are saved by **ENDURING** to the end (Matt.10:22).
16. We are saved by **FAITH** (Romans 3:28).

Alone?

The Scriptures say that we are saved by all of these things, but not by any one of them **alone**. For example, I Peter 3:21 states that we are saved by baptism. It would be just as reasonable to say that we are saved by baptism alone as it is to say we are saved by faith alone. Neither statement would be correct.

Even the person who says that one can be saved by faith alone is not consistent in his position, for he also believes that repentance is necessary for salvation. If one were saved the moment that he believes with nothing else required of him, then repentance would not be necessary. Faith and repentance are not the same thing. Faith is putting trust in the Lord and repentance is turning away from sin. Since sinners must repent before they can be forgiven of their sins (2 Cor. 7:10), salvation could not be by faith alone.

What about confessing the name of the Lord? If salvation is by faith only, then the sinner can be saved without confessing Christ. Paul said, *"With the mouth confession is made unto salvation"* (Rom. 10:10). The logical order would be for one to believe in Jesus, repent of his sins, and then confess Him. One would hardly confess Christ if he did not believe in Him. But, salvation does not come until the sinner confesses Christ. Therefore, salvation cannot be by faith alone.

Degrees of Faith

The Bible speaks of more than one degree of faith. Before one accepts the *"faith only"* position, he should look at these and see if it makes sense to attribute saving power to all of them:
1. There is a *"dead faith"* – James 2:26, *"For as the body without the spirit is dead, so faith without works is dead also."*
2. There is a *"little faith"* – Matt. 6:30, *"O you of little faith."*
3. There is a *"weak faith"* – Rom. 14:1, *"...one who is weak

in the faith."
4. There is a *"strong faith"* – Rom. 4:20, *"He was strengthened in faith."*
5. There is a *"great faith"* – Matt. 8:10, *"I have not found such great faith."*
6. There is a *"perfect faith"* – James 2:22, *"...And by faith was made perfect."*

Obviously, one can not be saved by a dead faith. But, a dead faith is simply a faith that is not accompanied by works, *"For as the body without the spirit is dead, so faith without works is dead also"* (James 2:26). Therefore, to accept the position that one can be saved by faith alone is the same as saying that a dead faith will save.

All Who Believe Will NOT Be Saved

Did you know that the New Testament speaks of some who believed but were obviously not saved? In John 12:42-43 we read of some of the chief rulers who believed on Jesus, but they did not confess Jesus for fear that they would be put out of the synagogue. Surely no one would contend that these men were saved. Believing alone was not enough.

In James 2:19 we read a startling statement about the demons. They believed! *"You believe there is one God. You do well. Even the demons believe and tremble."* If faith only will save, are we to conclude that the demons are also saved? Of course not! Faith alone will not save.

In Acts chapter 26 we read about King Agrippa. This case leaves no doubt that one can be a believer and yet not be a Christian. When Paul appeared before Agrippa he preached to him, relating his own conversion to Christ. He told him about the crucified and resurrected Christ. He emphasized that Moses and the prophets had foretold of these things in the gospel. Paul asked, *"King Agrippa, do you believe the prophets? I know that you do believe"* (v. 27). Agrippa replied, *"You almost persuade me to become a Christian"* (v. 28). Agrippa was a believer but was not convinced to become a Christian. Faith alone did not save him.

James, in James 2:26, discusses faith alone, a faith that found no expression in works, and concludes that such a faith is dead. Faith without works is an incomplete faith. James 2:22 states, *"Do you see that faith was working together with his works, and by works faith was made perfect?"*

What Kind of Faith Saves?

There is no question that faith saves, but what kind of faith is it? The faith that saves is an obedient faith. God has never rewarded an inactive or disobedient faith. Even under the Old Testament, first there was faith, then obedience, then God's blessing. The eleventh chapter of Hebrews gives us several examples of an obedient faith. It was by faith that Abel offered a more excellent sacrifice than did Cain (Heb. 11:4). Noah had faith in God and it was his faith that caused him to obey God and construct an ark (Heb. 11:7). It was Abraham's faith in God that made him willing to offer up his son Isaac on the alter (Heb. 11:17). It was by faith that the Israelites obeyed God's instructions and the walls of Jericho fell down after they were encircled for seven days (Heb. 11:30). In each case the blessing would not have been given had the faith not been expressed in obedience.

Faith Must Be Obedient

In the all-important matter of becoming a Christian, the principle remains true. A saving faith is one that is active and obedient. Jesus said, *"But why do you call me 'Lord, Lord,' and not do the things which I say?"* (Luke 6:46). Peter declared, *"In truth I perceive that God shows no partiality. But in every nation whoever fears Him and works righteousness is accepted by Him"* (Acts 10:34-35). Paul said, *"For in Christ Jesus neither circumcision nor uncircumcision avails anything, but faith working through love"* (Gal. 5:6).

In order for faith to be valid it must find expression in obedience. I Peter 4:17 clearly makes the point that the gospel must be obeyed: *"For the time has come for judgment to begin at the house of God; and if it begins with us first, what will be the end of those who do not obey the gospel of God."* Paul put it this way: *"... in flaming fire taking vengeance on those who do not know God, and on those who do not obey the gospel of our Lord Jesus Christ."*

Faith Alone Was Not Enough for the 3,000 on the Day of Pentecost

Let us notice in chapter 2 of the book of Acts the first example of believers becoming Christians. The first gospel sermon was preached in which the people were told that they had crucified the Son of God (v. 36). The people were obviously believers as they were cut to the heart by what they heard. They said to Peter and the rest of the apostles, *"Men and brethren, what shall we do?"* (v. 37).

These believers had not yet received the forgiveness of their sins. They were not yet Christians. They were not yet members of the Lord's church, but they did believe! More was required of them than believing. When the people asked what to do to be saved, Peter replied by saying, *"Repent, and let every one of you be baptized in the name of Jesus Christ for the remission of sins..."* (v. 38). About three thousand people *"gladly received his word"* (v. 41). *"The Lord added to the church daily those who were being saved"* (v. 47). We must see the Biblical order:

1. Faith resulted from hearing the gospel preached.
2. Repentance and baptism was commanded to those who believed.
3. When they obeyed by repenting and being baptized,
4. They received the forgiveness of sins. Forgiveness was not given until after baptism.
5. The saved were then added to the church.

These people were not saved by faith only. Salvation did not occur until after baptism. Had there been no obedience there would have been no forgiveness of sins. Peter knew nothing about the modern teaching of salvation occurring the moment of believing.

"Unto Salvation"

The foregoing is in harmony with the teaching of Paul in Romans 10:17, *"So then faith comes by hearing, and hearing by the word of God."* Also in Romans 10:10 Paul declared, *"For with the heart one believes unto righteousness and with the mouth confession is made unto salvation."* Belief or faith is produced from hearing the Word of God. Belief is *"unto righteousness."* This faith moves one to confess the Lord, which is *"unto salvation."* Obviously, Paul knew nothing of salvation occurring the moment one believes. The three thousand believers were baptized and became Christians by their obedient faith. Their faith was manifested by their obedience to the Lord's commands.

Faith Alone Was Not Enough for the Ethiopian

In Acts chapter 8 we read about the conversion of a man from Ethiopia. Philip *"preached Jesus to him"* (v. 35). As they continued traveling they came to some water and the Ethiopian said, *"See, here is water. What hinders me from being baptized?"* (v. 36). It is interesting to note that we are only told that *"Jesus"* was preached to the man, and yet at the first opportunity the man wanted to be baptized. Philip told him that he could be baptized if he believed with all of his heart. The Ethiopian eunuch answered and said, *"I believe that Jesus Christ is the Son of God"* (v. 37). *"So he commanded the chariot to stand still, and both Philip and the eunuch went down into the water, and he baptized him"* (v. 38). Even though the Ethiopian eunuch believed, he knew that more was required of him than just believing. After making the confession of his belief in Jesus he was immersed in water by Philip. When he came up out of the water the eunuch went on his way rejoicing.

Faith Alone Was Not Enough for the Philippian Jailer

Advocates of the *"faith only"* position almost always go to the conversion of the Philippian jailer, recorded in the 16th chapter of the book of Acts, in order to prove their doctrine. A closer look at this case will clearly show that *"faith only"* is not the teaching of the passage.

There was a great earthquake in the prison at Philippi and the jail doors were opened. The jailer was about to kill himself, thinking that the prisoners had escaped, but Paul told him to do himself no harm. The jailer then fell down before Paul and Silas and said, *"Sirs, what must I do to be saved?"* (v. 30). Paul and Silas responded by saying, *"Believe on the Lord Jesus Christ, and you will be saved, you and your household"* (v. 31). Many who teach *"faith only"* want to stop at the end of verse 31, but this does an injustice to the passage.

Paul and Silas were about to introduce to the jailer the only One in the entire world who could give him salvation. At this point the jailer did not believe in Jesus. Before the jailer had the opportunity to hear the Word, he asked what he needed to do to be saved. Paul and Silas told him, *"Believe in the Lord Jesus, and you shall be saved."*

Please notice that Paul and Silas did not say *"believe only."* He was told to believe because salvation always begins with believing. The jailer could not believe in Jesus until he was taught about Him (Rom. 10:14). Telling the jailer to believe in Jesus was not the end of the discussion. It was the beginning! Please notice the very next verse: *"And they spoke the Word of the Lord to him together with all who were in his house"* (v. 32). How could the jailer possibly believe until the Word of the Lord was spoken to him. When Paul and Silas taught the jailer about the Lord he did believe. Now notice what the believing jailer did, *"And immediately he was baptized, he and all his household"* (v. 33).

When the *"Word of the Lord"* was declared, the jailer believed. But, something in addition to believing in Jesus was required of him. He was baptized. When the *"Word of the Lord"* was preached, it included baptism. If the jailer had only believed he would not have received the forgiveness of his sins.

Faith Only Was
Not Enough for Saul of Tarsus

In chapters 9, 16, and 26 of Acts is found the amazing conversion of Saul of Tarsus (later to be called Paul). Saul had been a violent persecutor of Christians. When Jesus appeared to him on the way to Damascus he was stricken blind. When Saul asked *"What shall I do, Lord?"* (Acts 22:10), he was told by Jesus to go into Damascus, *"And there you will be told of all that has been appointed for you to do"* (Acts 22:11).

Saul was taken into Damascus where he prayed and went without food or drink for three days. Most certainly Saul was a believer. He showed signs of believing and repentance by his praying and fasting, and yet he still was not saved. He had not been forgiven of his sins. In Damascus he was told by Ananias what he must do in order to be saved. He told Saul about the Lord and concluded by saying, *"And now why do you delay? Arise and be baptized, and wash away your sins, calling on His name"* (Acts 22:16). Saul's sins were not washed away when he first believed. It was not until he submitted to Christ in baptism that he was he saved.

Those Who Believe
Have "Right" to Become Christians

According to John 1:11-12 believing in Jesus is still short of being a child of God. *"He came to His own, and His own did not receive Him. But as many as received Him, to them He gave the right to become children of God, to those who believe in his name."* The New King James Version translates verse 12 this way: *"To them gave he power to become the sons of God, even to them that believe on his name."*

The one who believes in Jesus is not already a child of God, but as the NKJV puts it, he has the power to become such because of his belief. One cannot become a child of God without believing in Jesus, but everyone who believes in Jesus does not choose to become a child of God. His faith must cause him to be obedient unto salvation.

Child of God through Faith

Paul told the Galatian Christians, *"For you are all sons of God through faith in Christ Jesus. For as many of you as were baptized into Christ have put on Christ."* Faith is the avenue to Christ. It is not faith only, but through faith that one gets into Christ. One does not get into Christ through simply believing in Christ, but his faith causes him to obey the Lord in baptism and thus he gets into Christ. One is not a child of God who is not in Christ.

"He Who Believes and Is Baptized"

Believing in Jesus will cause one to want to obey Him in whatever He requires. In Mark 16:16 Jesus joins faith and baptism together and says that they result in salvation. If one desires to be saved, simply believing will not be enough. The one who believes will then be baptized. *"He who believes and is baptized will be saved; but he who does not believe will be condemned."*

Those who teach that salvation comes at the point of believing must change Mark 16:16 to read *"He who believes and is not baptized will be saved."* To alter the Scriptures does not change the plan of salvation. What Jesus said is still true and salvation will not come to one who only believes.

"He Who Does Not Believe"

Some try to make the latter part of verse 16 nullify the need for baptism, *"But he who does not believe will be condemned."* In no way does that passage nullify what Jesus has just said. It simply states the obvious that if one does not believe he will certainly not be baptized or do anything else to please the Lord. It was not necessary for the Lord to say, *"He who does not believe and is not baptized will be condemned."* A doctor may say to his patient, *"If you eat your food and digest it you will live. If you do not eat you will die."* It certainly would not be necessary for the doctor to say, *"If you do not eat your food and do not digest it you will die."* The patient could not digest his food if he didn't eat. The person who does not believe would have no interest in being baptized. The Lord meant what he said. He promises salvation to those who not only believe but are baptized as well.

Comprehensive Faith

In the Bible faith is often used in the comprehensive sense and includes trust and obedience. For example, John 3:16 states, *"That whoever believes in Him should not perish but have everlasting life."* John 3:36 states, *"He who believes in the Son has everlasting life."* These verses do not teach that the sinner can be saved by faith only. Other scriptures clearly show that repentance, confession, and baptism are necessary parts of the entire process of receiving salvation in Christ. In these verses *"believes"* includes everything involved in coming to Christ and remaining faithful to Him.

It does a terrible injustice to such passages to insert the word *"only"* before the world *"believe,"* suggesting that obedience to the Lord is not important and is not necessary for salvation. If the Lord had wanted the word *"only"* to be there, he would have put it in the text, but it is not there.

"For by Grace..."

Ephesians 2:8-9 states, *"For by grace you have been saved through faith, and that not of yourselves; it is the gift of God, not of works, lest anyone should boast."* We need to be reminded that it is by God's grace that we are saved, and no one can be saved except by grace. God's grace through Jesus Christ has been extended to all men (Titus 2:11). But not all have accepted the expression of God's love.

If God's grace were the only consideration, then all would be saved, but those who reject Jesus will be lost (Mark 16:16). Salvation is not by grace only. Our obedience is necessary, but after we have obeyed all that he has asked of us, we still have not deserved salvation and it is still by his goodness, kindness, mercy, and grace that we are saved. Those who through an obedient faith and by God's grace have been saved still have nothing about which to boast. They have not earned their salvation by their obedience to Him.

You Can Be Saved

If you are not a child of God you need to respond to God's love, mercy, and grace. If you believe in Jesus as God's Son (John 8:24) you do well, but if you will be saved, you also need to repent of your sins (2 Pet. 3:9). Repentance is a change of mind that brings about a change of direction in your life. Faith and repentance are vital parts of the plan of salvation, but there is more. You will also want to confess your faith in Jesus as the Son of God (Rom. 10:10). Sadly, many do not proceed with the plan of salvation any further than this. They stop short of receiving the forgiveness of sins and stop short of becoming true children of God. After one believes, repents, and confesses Christ, what is lacking? To complete your obedience to the gospel you must be buried (immersed) in the water of baptism (Acts 2:38, I Peter 3:21).

When you have been baptized you will have been **buried with Christ** (Col. 2:12). You will arise from baptism having your **sins washed away** (Acts 22:16). You will have **clothed yourself in Christ** (Gal. 3:27). You will be **in Christ** (Rom. 6:3). You will be **saved** and be a **member of the church** that we read about in the New Testament (I Peter 3:21, Acts 2:47). You will arise to **walk in newness of life** (Romans 6:4).

CHAPTER 4
WHAT IS OUR AUTHORITY IN RELIGION?

Authority Is Necessary

We must have standards of authority in all phases of our lives. Every nation must have some form of authority or government. Without this, chaos would result. We have standards in weights and measures. If we didn't have these we could not agree on the length of a yard or what it takes to make a pound. If we had no standards in our monetary system we could not agree on the worth of a quarter, or how many quarters it would take to make a dollar. If we had no standards for time keeping every person would have a different time. Standards are all around us, and are absolutely necessary to our well being.

What About Authority in Religion?

Of all areas of authority, what could be more important than recognizing the proper authority in religion? Pleasing God is far more important than everyone agreeing on the time of day. In the religious world today we have hundreds of religious bodies teaching different things, yet all claiming to be right. On what basis can right or wrong be determined? Right and wrong can only be determined by using an absolute standard of authority.

Division Is the Result of Having No Authority

As a result of not adhering to the proper standard of authority the so-called *"Christian"* world is horribly divided. Sadly, some who choose the wrong standard of authority even take pride in there being so many different churches. In contrast, Paul pleaded for unity. *"Now I plead with you, brethren, by the name of our Lord Jesus Christ, that you all speak the same thing, and that there be no divisions among you, but that you be perfectly joined together in the same mind and in the same judgment"* (NKJV) (I Cor. 1:10). Jesus himself prayed that all of his followers would be one. *"I do not pray for these alone, but also for those who will believe in Me through their word; that they all may be one, as You, Father, are in Me, and I in you; that they also may be one in Us, that the world may believe that You sent me."* (John 17:20-21).

The religious world can never be united until we all accept the same standard of authority. If we do not agree on the same authority we cannot determine what is right to teach, nor can we know how to worship. What is the correct standard of authority in religion? Let us first approach this question negatively and observe several common standards that are not correct.

What About Allowing Our Feelings to Be the Authority?

The way one feels cannot be a safe authority for what he practices religiously. He may feel something is perfectly good, when in reality it is actually evil. Merely believing something to be true does not make it true. Unfortunately, many base their religious practices on their own subjective feelings. Since it feels good to them, they are convinced that they are right.

Feelings can be very deceptive. Saul of Tarsus was sure that he was right in persecuting Christians, but he was dead wrong. He did this with a clear conscience, *"Then Paul, looking earnestly at the council, said, 'Men and brethren, I have lived in all good conscience before God until this day'"* (Acts 23:1). But, his conscience misled him. He felt right about his wrongdoing until he learned the truth.

The brothers of Joseph sold him into slavery and allowed their father to believe he had been killed (Gen. 37:31-33). Jacob grieved for years as if his son had actually been killed, but his feelings deceived him. Sadly, many feel that their sins have been remitted, but their feelings have deceived them.

Does the Church Have the Authority to Make Binding Decisions?

Many sincere people accept as binding authority whatever their church dictates. Is this Biblical? No, the church of the New Testament was not given authority to meet in conferences, conventions or synods to make decisions that were binding on Christians. In the United States we have several hundred religious bodies meeting annually to make decisions about that for which they will stand, as well as that which they will believe. Each church differs from every other religious group. From a Biblical standpoint, which of these decisions is binding upon Christians? The answer is none of them!

Regardless of how large the convention or conference may be, it is still composed of mere men. The items of belief that are established are just doctrines of men, and as such, they have no merit. *"And in vain they worship me, teaching as doctrines the commandments of men"* (Matt. 15:9). Typical of the doctrines established by men, they are ever subject to the change of future councils, who may consider them outdated and unappealing. Fortunately, there is an authority for Christians, but it is not to be found in the councils of men.

What About Creeds?

Many honest and sincere people allow their church creed to be their authority in religion. All creeds written by men either contain too much or too little. If they contain less than the Bible, they contain too little. If they contain more than the Bible, they contain too much, and require that which is not required in the Bible. If a creed disagrees with the Bible it obviously is wrong. Paul said, *"That you may learn in us not to think beyond what is written..."* (I Cor. 4:6). Creeds are not only unnecessary, they are divisive. Unity among those who claim to believe in Christ can never be a reality as long as each body has its own distinctive creed.

Can One Man Be the Infallible Guide?

Some are content to allow one man to be the head of their church, and as such to be the infallible guide for all members of that church. Such an arrangement is absolutely unknown to the Bible. Jesus never gave up his position as head of the church to any man. *"And he is the head of the body, the church, who is the beginning, the firstborn from the dead, that in all things he may have the preeminence"* (Col. 1:18). God never intended to give to Peter, Paul, or any other human being the power to rule over his church. Furthermore, no man is infallible, *"For all have sinned and fall short of the glory of God"* (Rom. 3:23).

What About Allowing Majority Rule to Be the Authority?

The voice of the majority is usually a fine thing in a democratic government, but majority rule does not establish authority in religion. Even if everyone is practicing a certain thing, it may still be wrong. The Lord Jesus Himself taught us this principle, *"Enter in by the narrow gate; for wide is the gate and broad is the way that leads to destruction and there are many who go in by it"* (Matt. 7:13). It has never been safe to follow the crowd. Even in the Old Testament the Lord said, *"You shall not follow a crowd to do evil"* (Ex. 23:2). We must look beyond "everybody agrees" when it comes to religious matters.

Can Family Loyalty Be the Authority in Religion?

One's family religion, past or present, cannot be the authority for what is done religiously. Paul was zealously following the religion of his family when he persecuted Christians and sent them to their deaths. His actions were wrong. When he learned the truth, he left the family religion and became a Christian (Acts 9:1-18).

Family is important, but it is not the final authority in religion. Jesus recognized there could be conflicts in this area, and stated that there is a higher priority than family. *"He who loves father or mother more than Me is not worthy of Me. And he who loves son or daughter more than me is not worthy of Me"* (Matt. 10:37). At the Judgment Day we will not be judged by the family standard, but by a much greater authority. *"So then each of us shall give account of himself to God"* (Rom. 14:12).

What About So-called Visions and Revelations?

Some misguided religious people today put their trust in those who claim to have had visions from heaven. Such so-called visions are not legitimate. Those who claim to have received such visions expose themselves as false teachers by claiming to have received a different doctrine than that contained in the New Testament. Even the angels of heaven were forbidden to preach a different doctrine than that which was preached by the apostles. Paul warned *"But even if we, or an angel from heaven, preach any other gospel to you than what we have preached to you, let him be accursed"* (Gal. 1:8). This places those who claim to have received visions with new and different doctrines in a very bad light.

Others claim to have had latter day revelations. Such claims must be questioned, for Jude declared, *"contend earnestly for the faith which was once for all delivered to the saints"* (Jude 3). Since the faith was *"once for all delivered"* there is no need for latter day revelations. Peter declared, *"as his divine power has given to us all things that pertain to life and godliness, through the knowledge of him who called us by glory and virtue"* (2 Peter 1:3). Since we have been furnished with *"all things that pertain to life and godliness"* there are no modern revelations.

The Positive Answer to the Question of Authority Is Jesus Christ

Having observed several areas that do not provide authority in religion, we must now direct our attention to the true source of religious authority, Jesus Christ. Jesus said, *"All authority has been given to Me in heaven and on earth"* (Matt. 28:18). If all authority belongs to Jesus, there is no room for any individual to succeed him on earth as head over the church. It leaves no room for conferences, synods, and conventions to create new doctrines or alter that which He has taught.

Colossians 3:17 explicitly states, **"And whatever you do in word or deed, do all in the name of the Lord Jesus."** "In word" addresses our preaching and teaching. "In deed" refers to our practicing. All that we teach and do religiously must be in accordance with the teachings of Jesus. All that Jesus taught, and all authority that He possessed came from the Father (John 12:49-50).

Holy Spirit and Apostles

Jesus taught His apostles so they could teach others, but they were not left to rely on their memories alone. He gave them the Holy Spirit to aid them in their preaching and writing. The Holy Spirit was to guide them into all truth, to bring to their remembrance that which He had taught them, and to show them things to come (John 16:14). Paul declared this principle in Ephesians 3:5 when he spoke of receiving the mystery of Christ, **"as it has now been revealed by the Spirit to His holy apostles and prophets."**

Old and New Testaments

In determining authority from the Word of God we must clearly understand the difference between the Old and New Testaments. We do not turn to the Law of Moses in the Old Testament to determine what God requires of us today. We are not under the Old Law. The Bible itself makes a clear distinction between the Old and the New Covenants:

"Behold, the days are coming, says the Lord, when I will make a new covenant..." (Heb. 8:8). "And for this reason He is the Mediator of the new covenant by means of death... For where there is a testament, there must also of necessity be the death of the testator. For a testament is in force after men are dead, since it has no power at all while the testator lives. Therefore not even the first covenant was dedicated without blood" (Heb. 9:15-18). "He takes away the first that he may establish the second" (Heb. 10:9).

The laws of the Old Testament are not binding upon Christians. When Christ died on the cross He brought the Old Law to a conclusion and He ushered into effect the New Covenant. *"Having wiped out the handwriting of requirements that was against us, which was contrary to us. And He has taken it out of the way, having nailed it to the cross"* (Col. 2:14).

The Authority of Jesus Is Expressed in His Word

The authoritative Word, the New Testament, is the means by which the Lord's authority is expressed today. It must be our only standard of faith and practice. It is not subject to feelings, limited understanding, or the fallibility of human beings. It is an objective standard by which all teaching can be measured. In it we are provided with *"all things that pertain to life and godliness"* (2 Pet. 1:3).

The Written Word Is Truth

What we have in the written Word is not a truth, but the truth. John 16:13 states, *"However, when He, the Spirit of truth, has come, He will guide you into all truth; for He will not speak* on His own authority, but whatever He hears He will speak; and He will tell you things to come." When the Thessalonians received the Word, they recognized it as the truth from God. When we open our Bibles we also must recognize it as God's truth and the supreme authority in religion. First Thessalonians 2:13 says, *"When you received the word of God which you heard from us, you welcomed it not as the word of men, but as it is in truth, the word of God..."*

No Other Gospel

What the apostles preached is contained in the Word. Our preaching must conform to their preaching. Gal. 1:8 says, *"But even if we, or an angel from heaven, preach any other gospel to you than what we have preached to you, let him be accursed."*

The written Word did not come from the mind of man, but from the mind of God. That is why it is the absolute authority in religion. 2 Peter 1:21 declares, *"For prophecy never came by the will of man, but holy men of God spoke as they were moved by the Holy Spirit."*

Those who properly receive God's word will honor it as the authority for recognizing and defending the true faith. Jude 3 says, *"Beloved, while I was very diligent to write to you concerning our common salvation, I found it necessary to write to you exhorting you to contend earnestly for the faith which was once for all delivered to the saints."*

Absolute Authority

With the Scriptures being the absolute authority in religion, we have the means by which we can measure all doctrines, and thereby we can know whether a doctrine is from man or God. 2 Tim. 3:16-17 declares, *"All Scripture is given by inspiration of God, and is profitable for doctrine, for reproof, for correction, for instruction in righteousness."*

It is not good enough to preach something just because it sounds good, or because it makes people feel good. The oracles (utterances) of God are contained in the written Word. When we teach and preach we must do so within the confines of the written Word. I Pet. 4:11 states, *"If anyone speaks, let him speak as the oracles of God."*

At the Judgment

At the Judgment Day there will be an absolute standard by which we all will be judged. John 12:48 says, *"He who rejects Me, and does not receive My words, has that which judges him -- the word that I have spoken will judge him in the last day."*

Sadly, there are many religious teachers today who take lightly the matter of teaching things that are foreign to the written Word. They do not hesitate to change or even deny the very standard of all religious authority, the Word. The Lord does not take this lightly. Rev. 22:18-19 states, *"For I testify to everyone who hears the words of the prophecy of this book: If anyone adds to these things, God will add to him the plagues that are written in this book; and if anyone takes away from the words of the book of this prophecy, God shall take away his part from the Book of Life..."*

How Does the Word Authorize?

In a study of the New Testament we come to realize how the Scriptures authorize. Man learns the will of God by direct statements (including commands), approved examples, and necessary inferences. These are valid ways of learning God's will about essential obedience. Please notice each of these.

Authority from Direct Statements and Commands

In I Peter 3:21 we have a direct statement that tells us that baptism is essential: *"There is also an antitype which now saves us – baptism (not the removal of the filth of the flesh, but the answer of a good conscience toward God), through the resurrection of Jesus Christ."* John 8:24 has a direct statement about the necessity of believing in Jesus: *"For if you do not believe that I am He, you will die in your sins."* Paul gives us two direct statements that give us authority to teach that baptism is immersion: *"Buried with Him in baptism"* (Col. 2:12), and *"Therefore we were buried with Him through baptism"* (Rom. 6:3). Even though these are not stated in the *"command"* form, they are every bit as strong and binding as direct commands.

Direct Command

Falling under the heading of *"direct statement"* is the command. A direct command is an authoritative direction, an order to be obeyed. One example of a direct command is Acts 17:30: *"Truly, these times of ignorance God overlooked, but now commands all men everywhere to repent."* We clearly understand that repentance is essential if we will please the Lord. Another example is found in Acts 2:38: *"Repent, and let every one of you be baptized in the name of Jesus Christ for the remission of sins."* To *"repent and be baptized"* is a direct command. One cannot be pleasing to God who refuses to comply with what the Lord has ordered.

The Great Commission

Another example of a direct command is found in Matt. 28:19: *"Go therefore and make disciples of all nations, baptizing them in the name of the Father and of the Son and of the Holy Spirit."* The command is to go teach and to baptize those who are taught. There are many direct commands in the Word. Paul stated in I Cor. 14:37: *"The things which I write to you are the commandments of the Lord."*

Authority from Necessary Inference

A necessary inference is an inescapable conclusion based on the implications of evidence. (The speaker implies, the hearer infers.) The Bible does not tell us that one must be old enough to be baptized. However, before one can be baptized he must be taught (Matt. 28:19), and he must believe (Mk. 16:16). The purpose of baptism is for the remission of sins (Acts 2:38). Infants are not capable of being taught the Word, nor are they capable of believing the Word. Furthermore, they have no sins to remit. Therefore, we must reach the conclusion by necessary inference that infants are not scriptural subjects for baptism.

Immersion and Preaching Jesus

Since New Testament baptism is a burial (Romans 6:4, Col. 2:12), the unavoidable inference is that immersion is the only acceptable form of baptism. Sprinkling or pouring will not do. Preaching Jesus fully includes preaching baptism. In Acts 8:35-40 we read of a man who had heard only one gospel sermon, and the subject was "Jesus." When this man came to water he asked the preacher to baptize him. How did he know that baptism was required? We must infer that when Philip preached "Jesus" to him he included baptism in his teaching.

No Latter Day Revelations

The Bible doesn't specifically say that there will be no latter day revelations. However, Jude v. 3 says that the faith *"was <u>once for all delivered</u> to the saints,"* and 2 Peter 1:3 states that *"His divine power has given to us all things that pertain to life and godliness."* We must infer from such passages that there are no new revelations or communications.

Elders

The Bible does not say that an elder in the church cannot be a woman. However, I Tim. 3:2 says that the elder must be "the husband of one wife." We must conclude by inference, therefore, that women are excluded from the eldership.

Authority Is Established by Approved Examples

If the early Christians understood that they were required to do something, their example indicates that we, under similar circumstances, must also do the same thing. For example, Acts 5:29 states: *"But Peter and the other apostles answered and said, we ought to obey God rather than men."* There is no command here, but there is the example of Peter expressing what he understood that Christians must do. Under similar circumstances we are obligated to act in a similar way and obey God rather than men.

The Lord's Supper

Paul told the Corinthians, *"Imitate me, just as I imitate Christ"* (I Corinthians 11:1). Paul was present when the church at Troas assembled on the first day of the week to observe the Lord's Supper. *"Now on the first day of the week, when the disciples came together to break bread, Paul, ready to depart the next day, spoke to them and continued his message until midnight"* (Acts 20:7). Paul not only approved, but he also participated in the services. We follow this approved example and observe the Lord's Supper each and every week on the first day of the week.

Binding Examples

Binding examples have a clearly implied command lying behind them. The Lord had previously instituted the Lord's Supper as emblematic of His body and blood. He had commanded His disciples to eat and drink of it (Matthew 26:26-27). When the church was established the disciples *"continued steadfastly in the apostles' doctrine and fellowship, in the breaking of bread, and in prayers"* (Acts 2:42).

What About Expediency?

In carrying out a direct statement, a necessary inference, or an approved example, we can employ that which is expedient, as long as the act is right within itself. For example, we have the direct command to *"Go into all the world and preach the gospel to every creature"* (Mark 16:15). To carry out the command to *"go"* we can do so by automobile, boat, airplane, horseback, or any other means of travel. To obey the command to *"preach"* we are free to use the pulpit, radio, TV, house-to-house, the written Word, or any other method that does not violate Scripture.

Law of Exclusion

When instructions are given to do a certain thing, it is not necessary to follow those instructions with a list of everything that is not meant. When you give someone your address, it is not necessary to tell them all the addresses that are not yours. By giving the correct address you eliminate all other addresses.

An example of the law of exclusion in the New Testament is seen in the instructions regarding the Lord's Supper. The New Testament does not say, *"You shall not have hamburgers and coffee as elements in the Lord's Supper."* A positive command or approved example does not have to be followed with a list of things that are not allowed. The elements of the Lord's Supper are clearly specified as *"bread"* and *"fruit of the vine"* (Matthew 26:26-30). It was not necessary for the Lord to then list all the things that we could not use as elements. That list would be endless. By telling us what to include, this automatically excludes all else.

Vocal Music

Vocal music is one type of music and instrumental music is another. When it comes to music in New Testament worship we have been told the kind of music that we are to offer. That music was specified as **vocal**. *"Teaching and admonishing one another in psalms and hymns and spiritual songs, singing with grace in your hearts to the Lord"* (Colossians 3:16). It was not necessary for the Lord to then say *"You cannot use instrumental music."* When he told us that the kind of music he wanted was vocal, that excluded all else. We have authority for vocal music but we have no authority to offer any other kind of music.

The Final Word

All teaching and practice in religious matters must be in accordance with the New Testament. It is **the final word**. It is **the authority**. Tampering with the Word, altering it, watering it down, explaining it away, or rejecting it as the sole authority of God can only cause men to lose their souls. On the other hand, we can go to heaven by learning, accepting, believing, and obeying what we read in God's precious Word. We must accept the authority of God.

CHAPTER 5
WHY BE BAPTIZED?

The New Testament has a great amount to say on the subject of baptism. The word *"baptize"* or some form of the word appears more than 100 times in the New Testament. Many are surprised to learn that baptism is commanded as an act of obedience to the Lord.

The importance of baptism is clearly seen in the numerous examples of first century followers of Christ submitting to baptism. In spite of all this, there is sharp disagreement on the subject. There is disagreement over the *"form"* of baptism, why one should be baptized, and who should be baptized. In this chapter we will investigate those three areas in order to determine what the Bible teaches about this important subject.

What "Form" of Baptism?

Although we often hear the term *"form of baptism,"* there is actually only one correct baptism according to the New Testament. Some would like to believe that sprinkling or pouring is acceptable baptism, but New Testament baptism is immersion. Notice Paul's description of true baptism, *"Therefore we were buried with Him through baptism into death, that just as Christ was raised from the dead by the glory of the Father, even so we also should walk in newness of life"* (Romans 6:4, NKJV).

True Baptism Is Immersion in Water

The baptism that we teach and practice today must be exactly the same as the baptism of the New Testament. New Testament baptism was a burial in water. *"Can anyone forbid water, that these should not be baptized?"* (Acts 10:47). In the New Testament baptism was a going down into water, and a coming up out of the water. *"Now as they went down the road, they came to some water. And the eunuch said 'See, here is water. What hinders me from being baptized?' Then Philip said, 'If you believe with all your heart, you may.' And he answered and said, 'I believe that Jesus Christ is the Son of God.' So, he commanded the chariot to stand still. And both Philip and the eunuch went down into the water, and he baptized him. Now when they came up out of the water, the Spirit of the Lord caught Philip away so that the eunuch saw him no more."* (Acts 8:36-39).

Colossians 2:12 should remove all doubt as to the only scriptural form of baptism, *"Buried with him in baptism, in which you also were raised with him."* How could the Lord have made it any clearer? True baptism is immersion.

The original Greek word for baptize in the New Testament clearly defines baptism as being immersion. The Greek word is **"baptizo"** and it means *"to dip, immerse, or submerge."* There is no way that **"baptize"** could ever be correctly translated *"sprinkling"* or *"pouring."*

Many good and honest people just assume that the form of baptism can be sprinkling, pouring, or immersion. Such a conclusion cannot be valid since this most definitely is not taught in the Scriptures. The New Testament tells us that there is *"one baptism*" (Ephesians 4:5), and that one baptism is immersion in water.

Why Be Baptized?
Because Baptism Is Commanded

In answering the question, "*Why be baptized?*" we should first point out that according to the New Testament, baptism is not optional. It is commanded. When Jesus gave the Great Commission He commanded baptism: "*Go therefore and make disciples of all the nations, baptizing them in the name of the Father and of the Son and of the Holy Spirit*" (Matthew 28:19). When Peter had concluded his preaching to Cornelius and to those assembled with him, "*He commanded them to be baptized in the name of the Lord.*" (Acts 10:48). Acts 2:38 states the command in this way, "*Repent and let every one of you be baptized in the name of Jesus Christ.*" Acts 22:16 also states that baptism is a command, "*Arise and be baptized.*" It should be apparent to all that baptism is commanded, but what is the purpose of baptism.

Why Be Baptized?
Because at Baptism the Lord Removes Our Sins

Ananias commanded a very penitent Saul of Tarsus, "*Arise and be baptized, and wash away your sins, calling on the name of the Lord*" (Acts 22:16). The purpose of Saul's baptism was to have his sins taken away. That forgiveness did not take place when Saul simply believed. It did not take place even when he added repentance to his belief, but it did take place when this penitent believer was baptized. Jesus said, "*He who believes and is baptized will be saved*" (Mark 16:16).

Peter wrote, "*There is also an antitype which now saves*

us - baptism" (I Peter 3:21). We observed earlier that Peter commanded Cornelius to be baptized and in this passage he tells us why. Salvation occurs at the point of baptism. Baptism is exactly when the sins of Cornelius were forgiven. On the day of Pentecost those who listened to Peter preach about Jesus were cut to their hearts and cried out, *"Men and brethren what shall we do? Then Peter said to them, Repent, and let everyone of you be baptized in the name of Jesus for the remission of sins"* (Acts 2:37-38). Baptism stands between a believer and salvation from his past sins.

Why Be Baptized?
Because at Baptism We Enter the Church

Not only are we saved from our past sins at baptism, it is at this point that we are added to the Lord's church. *"And the Lord added to the church daily those who were being saved"* (Acts 2:47). Paul declared, *"For by one spirit we were all baptized into one body."* That one body is the church, *"And He is head of the body, the church"* (Colossians 1:18). *"And He put all things under His feet, and gave Him to be head over all things to the church, which is His body"* (Ephesians 1:22-23).

We do not join the church in the same sense that one joins a club. We do not become a part of the church of Christ by being voted in. At the time when one is scripturally baptized, the Lord takes care of that person's church membership by adding him to His church.

Why Be Baptized?
Because at Baptism We Enter into Christ

In Romans 6:3 Paul tells us, *"Or do you not know that as many of us as were baptized into Christ Jesus were baptized into His death?"* Being in Christ is essential, but did you know that the only way the New Testament tells us that we can get into Christ is by baptism? If one can be saved without baptism he can be saved without being in Christ. We must be in Christ to receive the benefits of His death.

Why Be Baptized?
Because at Baptism We Put on Christ

What logical person who desires to follow Christ would not do what he must do to put on Christ or to get into Christ? *"For as many of you as were baptized into Christ have put on Christ"* (Galatians 3:27). It is at the point of baptism that we are clothed in Him. We put Him on. For a responsible person to contend that one can be saved without baptism, he is saying in effect that one can be saved without putting on Christ.

Who Should Be Baptized?
Not Infants

Infant baptism is practiced so widely in the denominational world that we need to pay special attention to what the Bible says or does not say about this practice. Many may be shocked to learn that the Bible does not authorize infant baptism at all. When we answer the question, *"Who should be baptized?"* we will clearly see that baptism cannot be for infants.

Baptism Is for Sinners

"Arise and be baptized and wash away your sins, calling on the name of the Lord" (Acts 22:16). *"There is also an antitype*

which now saves us — baptism" (I Peter 3:21). *"Repent, and let every one of you be baptized in the name of Jesus Christ for the remission of sins"* (Acts 2:38). The Scriptures declare that baptism is for the remission of sins. Infants cannot be baptized since they are not sinners. They are born in innocence without sin. Sin is not hereditary. *"The son shall not bear the iniquity of the Father"* (Ezekiel 18:20). Sin is something we do, not something we inherit. *"Whoever commits sin also commits lawlessness, and sin is lawlessness"* (I John 3:4).

Sin is the transgression of God's law. How can infants transgress the law of God of which they know nothing? If children were depraved sinners, as some erroneously teach, Jesus would never have held them up as examples of purity and humility. He said, *"Of such is the kingdom of heaven"* (Matthew 19:14).

Baptism Is for Those Who Believe in Jesus

"He who believes and is baptized will be saved; but he who does not believe will be condemned" (Mark 16:16). In Acts 8:12 we see an example of those who were responding to the call of Christ, *"But when they believed Philip as he preached the things concerning the kingdom of God and the name of Jesus Christ, both men and women were baptized."* Baptism cannot be for infants since we are required to believe before we can be baptized, and infants are not capable of believing.

Baptism Is for Those Who Have Been Taught

Jesus commanded, *"Go therefore and make disciples of all the nations, baptizing them in the name of the Father and of the*

Son and of the Holy Spirit, teaching them to observe all things that I have commanded you, and lo, I am with you always, even to the end of the age"* (Matthew 28:19-20).

Baptism cannot be for infants since a candidate for baptism must be taught and infants are not capable of being taught the Word of God. Infants who are subjected to being *"baptized"* have no understanding of what is being done to them.

Baptism Is for Those Who Have Repented

"Repent and let every one of you be baptized in the name of Jesus Christ for the remission of sins" (Acts 2:38). Baptism cannot be for infants since the subject for baptism must repent. Infants are not capable of repenting and have no reason to repent. They are without sin. Repentance requires recognition of wrong and a turning away from it.

Baptism Is for Those Who are Willing to Obey

After Peter had declared the Word of the Lord to the household of Cornelius he then *"commanded them to be baptized in the name of the Lord"* (Acts 10:48). Those who have been taught should be eager to complete their primary obedience to the Lord by being baptized into Him. Obviously, an infant is not capable of understanding or obeying such a command. Baptism cannot be for infants.

Baptism Is for Those Who Have Confessed Their Faith in Jesus

Before the Ethiopian eunuch could be baptized it was necessary for him to confess Christ, *"And the eunuch said, 'See, here is water. What hinders me from being baptized?' Then Philip said, 'If you believe with all your heart you may,' and he answered and said, 'I believe that Jesus Christ is the Son of God'"* (Acts 8:36-37).

In Romans 10:9-10 we learn that confession is made, leading to salvation, *"That if you confess with your mouth the Lord Jesus and believe in your heart that God has raised Him from the dead, you will be saved. For with the heart one believes unto righteousness and with the mouth confession is made unto salvation."* Baptism cannot be for infants since candidates for baptism are required to confess their faith in Jesus. Infants are obviously not capable of confessing Jesus.

Baptism Is for Those Who Are Accountable

All children are born without sin, but they reach an age of accountability when they are responsible for their sins. *"You were perfect in your ways from the day you were created, till iniquity was found in you"* (Ezekiel 28:15). A child reaches this age when he is old enough to know the difference in right and wrong and is able by his own will to turn from sin to Christ. Until this age is achieved, all children are safe and therefore do not need to be saved.

Are There Examples of Infant Baptism in the New Testament?

No. In all of the New Testament there is not a single example of an infant being baptized. Nowhere are parents instructed to bring their infants to be baptized. Baptism was never intended for infants.

Who Then Should Be Baptized?

Baptism is for those who need to have their sins forgiven, *"Then Peter said to them, 'Repent, and let every one of you be baptized in the name of Jesus Christ for the remission of sins, and you shall receive the gift of the Holy Spirit'"* (Acts 2:38), *"And now why are you waiting? Arise and be baptized and wash away your sins, calling on the name of the Lord"* (Acts 22:16), *"There is also an antitype which now saves us — baptism (not the removal of the filth of the flesh, but the answer of a good conscience toward God), through the resurrection of Jesus Christ"* (I Peter 3:21).

Baptism is for those who believe in Jesus, *"He who believes and is baptized will be saved, but he who does not believe will be condemned"* (Mark 16:16). *"But when they believed Philip as he preached things concerning the kingdom of God and the name of Jesus Christ, both men and women were baptized"* (Acts 8:12).

Baptism is for those who have been taught, *"And Jesus came and spoke to them, saying, 'All authority has been given to Me in heaven and on earth. Go therefore and make disciples of all the nations, baptizing them in the name of the Father and of the Son and of the Holy Spirit"* (Matthew 28:18-20).

Baptism is for those who have repented, *"Repent, and let every one of you be baptized in the name of Jesus Christ for the remission of sins..."* (Acts 2:38)

It is for those who are willing to obey the Lord, *"He who believes and is baptized shall be saved, but he who does not believe will be condemned"* (Mark 16:16). *"And he commanded them to be baptized in the name of the Lord"* (Acts 10:48).

It is for those who have confessed Jesus, *"Now as they went *down the road, they came to some water. And the eunuch said, 'See, here is water. What hinders me from being baptized?' Then Philip said, 'If you believe with all your heart, you may.' And he answered and said, ' I believe that Jesus Christ is the Son of God. So he commanded the chariot to stand still. And both Philip and the eunuch went down into the water, and he baptized him"* (Acts 8:36-38). "That if you confess with your mouth the Lord Jesus and believe in your heart that God has raised Him from the dead you will be saved. For with the heart one believes unto righteousness and with the mouth confession is made unto salvation" (Romans 10:9-10). Baptism is for responsible, accountable individuals.

Conclusion

Baptism is vitally important because God commands it. It stands between one who believes in Jesus and the forgiveness of sins. It stands between condemnation and life everlasting. The one who wants a proper relationship with God will want to put Jesus on in the waters of baptism and be added by the Lord to His church.

CHAPTER 6
WHAT IS THE "ONE BAPTISM"?

The Christian's *"Seven-fold Platform for Unity"* is found in Ephesians 4:4-6: *"There is one body and one Spirit, just as you were called in one hope of your calling; one Lord, one faith, one baptism, one God and Father of all who is above all and through all and in you all"* (NKJV).

You will notice that there are seven words, each of which is preceded by the word *"one"*. Please give special attention to the expression *"one baptism."* When some of our brethren went to Japan shortly after World War II ended, they had a great deal of difficulty in convincing the people that there was only one true God. Reportedly, they had 600 million gods, more gods than people. In the United States the difficulty is not usually in convincing people that there is one God, but there is much difficulty in convincing some that there is one baptism.

In the cited text we learn that there is *"one God."* We accept that limited number, for after all, *"one God"* is exactly what the Word says. Why then should there be any difficulty in accepting the fact that there is *"one baptism?"* The same text that tells us there is *"one"* God also tells us there is "one" baptism. When the Bible says that there is "one" God and *"one"* baptism we can know for a certainty that there are just as many true baptisms as there are true Gods. Since the number is unquestionably clear when applied to the number of Gods, it must also be just as clear when that number is applied to the number of baptisms.

The person who believes there is only *"one"* God does well. When he wants to show proof of the Bible teaching as to the number of true Gods, he turns to the passage under consideration and concentrates his attention on Ephesians 4:6 which states there is *"One God and Father of all..."* However, having established that there is only *"one"* God, the same person, because of a preconceived idea about baptism, may totally ignore verse 5 of the same passage which clearly says *"one baptism"* and then teach that there is a plurality of valid baptisms today. Whatever the passage means regarding the number of true Gods, it means that we have that same number of valid baptisms.

What About the Holy Spirit Baptism?

Someone might suggest that the *"one"* baptism is the baptism of the Holy Spirit. This just couldn't be the *"one"* baptism that we are looking for because of what the New Testament reveals about Holy Spirit baptism:

1. The Holy Spirit baptism was for a specific purpose, to enable the recipients to perform miraculous signs.
2. The Holy Spirit baptism was for a specific time, during the infancy of the church.
3. The Holy Spirit baptism was for a specific people, namely, the apostles, and the household of Cornelius (Acts 2, Acts 10).
4. The Holy Spirit baptism was never commanded, but only promised (Acts 1:8).
5. The Holy Spirit baptism could not be administered by men, but only by Jesus (Matthew 3:11-12).

It should be obvious to all that the baptism of the Holy Spirit cannot be the "one" baptism. We are looking for a baptism that was commanded for all people for all time, and one that could be administered by men in the name of the Father, Son, and Holy Spirit.

Are There Three Baptisms?

Your dictionary may say that there are three baptisms: immersion, sprinkling, and pouring. Obviously, the writer of the dictionary definition is only reporting what is being practiced by various religious groups. No effort is made by the dictionary to define the word as it is used in the Bible. Therefore, we do not go to the dictionary to learn about the "one" baptism. If the "one" baptism is sprinkling, then pouring and immersion are excluded. If the "one" baptism is immersion, then sprinkling and pouring are excluded. Whatever the "one" baptism is, keep in mind that only "one" is authorized by God. Every other baptism except that "one" is in error.

The Baptism of the Great Commission

To correctly identify the "one" baptism, we must find the baptism that was intended to continue from Pentecost to the end of the world. In giving the Great Commission Jesus said: *"Go therefore and make disciples of all the nations, baptizing them in the name of the Father and of the Son and of the Holy Spirit, teaching them to observe all things that I commanded you; and lo, I am with you always, even to the end of the age"* (Matthew 28:19-20).

That preaching and baptizing began on the day of Pentecost

as the church was ushered into existence. It is the baptism of the Great Commission that is valid today, and will continue to be valid until the end of time. It was commanded. It was to be administered by men. It was for the people of all nations who were capable of believing (Mark 16:16).

The Baptism of the Great Commission Was in Water

"Now as they went down the road, they came to some water; and the eunuch said, 'See, here is water. What hinders me from being baptized?' Then Philip said, 'If you believe with all your heart, you may.' And he answered and said, 'I believe that Jesus Christ is the Son of God.'" (Acts 8:36-37). There was enough water for the one who was being baptized, as well as the one who was doing the baptizing, to go down into the water. This was not a *"sprinkling"* or a *"pouring."* Clearly it was a burial, an immersion. *"So he commanded the chariot to stand still; and both Philip and the eunuch went down into the water, and he baptized him. Now when they came up out of the water, the Spirit of the Lord caught Philip away..."* (Acts 8:38-39).

The "One" Baptism Was a Burial

It was the apostle Paul who wrote in Ephesians 4:5 that there is only *"one"* baptism. Clearly, he understood what the *"one"* baptism was. In Romans 6:4 he described it as a burial:

"Therefore we were buried with Him through baptism into death, in order that just as Christ was raised from the dead by the glory of the Father, even so we also should walk in newness of life."

Again, it was Paul who described the *"one"* baptism to the

Colossians: *"Buried with Him in baptism, in which you also were raised with Him through faith in the working of God, who raised Him from the dead"* (Colossians 2:12). Without question, the *"one"* baptism was a burial in water.

Sprinkling and Pouring Must Be Excluded

There are three distinct words used in the Greek for *"sprinkling," "pouring,"* and *"immersion."* The word for *"sprinkle"* is *"rantizo."* The word for *"pour"* is *"keo."* The word for *"baptize"* is *"baptizo."* When the English bible was produced, the Greek word *"baptizo"* was not translated. Instead, it was anglicized or transliterated. It was carried over from the Greek by changing the final letter from *"o"* to *"e."* If the word had been translated properly, there would be no question as to the so-called *"mode"* of baptism.

Acts 2:38 would correctly say: *"Repent and let every one of you be immersed in the name of Jesus Christ for the remission of sins."* Mark 16:16 would say: *"He who believes and is immersed will be saved."* John the *"baptist"* would be John the *"immerser."* The Greek words for *"sprinkling"* and *"pouring"* are not to be found in these passages because the subject is baptism, and baptism means *"immersion."*

The "One" Baptism Was for the Remission of Sins

When Peter stood up with the other apostles on the day of Pentecost and preached the gospel for the first time, the plan of salvation was revealed. Those who wanted to be saved were commanded to repent and be baptized. The purpose of that baptism was *"For the remission of sins"* (Acts 2:38). At the time of Paul's conversion the preacher not only instructed him to be baptized, he also told him the purpose of that baptism: *"Arise and be baptized and wash away your sins, calling on the name of the Lord"* (Acts 22:16). Today, in order for a baptism to be the *"one"* true and valid baptism, it must be for the same purpose, the remission of sins.

Description of the "One" Baptism

Putting together what we have learned from these Bible passages, the following is a description of the *"one"* baptism that is valid today:

1. The *"one"* baptism is water (Acts 8:36).
2. The *"one"* baptism is a burial in water and a resurrection from the water (Romans 6:4, Acts 8:38-39).
3. The *"one"* baptism is to be administered by men (Matthew 28:19).
4. The *"one"* baptism is to last until the end of time (Matthew 28:20).
5. The *"one"* baptism is for the people of the whole world (Matt. 28:19, Mark 16:15).
6. The *"one"* baptism is to be done in the name of the Father, Son, and Holy Spirit (Matthew 8:19).
7. The *"one"* baptism is for the forgiveness of sins (Acts 22:16, Acts 2:38).
8. The *"one"* baptism is for those who are capable of believing (Mark 16:16).

Conclusion

Any baptism that does not fit the description above cannot be the *"one"* baptism of the New Testament. But, what about those people who thought they were being baptized in the Holy Spirit? What about those people who have had water poured or sprinkled on them? It simply means that they have never been baptized as the Bible teaches.

What should they do? Let the Bible answer the question: ***"Repent and let every one of you be baptized in the name of Jesus Christ for the remission of sins; and you shall receive the gift of the Holy Spirit"*** (Acts 2:38).

CHAPTER 7
IS THE BIBLE FROM GOD OR MAN?

There is a great battle raging against the Bible. Relentless enemies of the Bible scoff at it, and laugh at those who believe that it came from God. Unfortunately, many reject the Bible without giving consideration to the wealth of evidence in favor of the Bible's credibility and divine authorship. To the unbiased and honest seeker of truth, this evidence is overwhelming. In this chapter we will present solid reasons to believe that the Bible is God's infallible, holy, divinely inspired Word.

The Bible Claims Inspiration

The Bible makes bold, unmistakable claims to inspiration. In 2 Tim. 3:16 Paul declared, *"All Scripture is given by inspiration of God, and is profitable for doctrine, for reproof, for correction, for instruction in righteousness"* (NKJV). There is no room for a person to say he believes the Bible but denies that it is inspired of God.

The fact of Biblical inspiration is clearly stated by the apostle Peter: *"Knowing this first, that no prophecy of Scripture is of any private interpretation, for prophecy never came by the will of man, but holy men of God spoke as they were moved by the Holy Spirit"* (2 Pet. 1:20-21).

The Greek word underlying the word *"inspiration"* means *"God-breathed."* God actually breathed out the Scriptures. The Bible is God's words. In the Old Testament alone there are over 2,000 phrases such as *"The Word of the Lord came unto Jonah," "God spoke to Moses,"* and *"God said."* The Bible views itself as being the Word of God. The fact that God used men as instruments to convey those words does not change the source.

On the day of Pentecost Peter stood up among the disciples and stated, *"Men and brethren, this Scripture had to be fulfilled, which the Holy Spirit spoke before by the mouth of David concerning Judas..."* (Acts 1:16). Peter then quoted from Psalms. Peter believed what David wrote was from the Holy Spirit and was therefore *"Scripture."*

Verbal Inspiration

The inspiration that the Bible claims for itself is *"verbal"* inspiration. The Apostle Paul claimed verbal inspiration: *"And my speech and my preaching were not with persuasive words of human wisdom, but in demonstration of the Spirit and of power"* (I Cor 2:4). In verse 7 Paul identifies the source of his words: *"But we speak the wisdom of God in a mystery, the hidden wisdom which God ordained before the ages for our glory."*

Infallible, Inerrant, Plenary

The Bible's inspiration is *"infallible"* and *"inerrant,"* meaning that it is completely trustworthy and free from errors and mistakes characteristic of uninspired writings. The inspiration of the Bible is also *"plenary,"* meaning that its inspiration extends to all of its parts. *"For this reason we also thank God without ceasing, because when you received the word of God which you heard from us, you welcomed it not as the word of men, but as it is in truth, the word of God"* (I Thess. 2:13).

The Bible came from God through Holy Spirit inspired men. We will examine ten lines of evidence that will verify this truth.

(1) The Bible Is Indestructible

The Bible has weathered the test of time. It is the most attacked book that has ever been written. In spite of these continual assaults, the Bible has not only survived, but it has consistently triumphed over its enemies. The enemies of the Bible attempted to destroy the Bible by force. As early as AD 303 the Emperor Diocletian issued an edict that every copy of the Bible was to be burned. He butchered so many Christians and destroyed so many Bibles that he was certain that he had exterminated Christianity. Down through the centuries similar enemies attempted to destroy the Bible by burning every copy they found. Those enemies are gone, but the Bible lives on.

The so-called *"higher critics"* such as Wolf, Cant, Semler, and Bauer tried to teach the Bible out of existence. These men are gone and all but forgotten, but the Bible continues to live.

Noted atheists of the past such as Voltaire, Thomas Paine, and Robert Ingersoll were certain that they could ridicule and laugh the Bible out of existence. Voltaire, Paine, and Ingersoll are gone, but the Bible lives on. Voltaire once boasted that *"In another hundred years there will not be another copy of the Bible on the face of the earth."* Just a few short years after Voltaire made this boast the Geneva Bible Society was using the Voltaire printing press to turn out thousands of Bibles! The very house where Voltaire once lived was used as a storehouse for Bibles.

Thomas Paine in his "Age of Reason" predicted that the Bible would be out of print within his lifetime. He stated, "**When I get through, there will not be five Bibles left in America. Within one hundred years, Bibles will be found only in museums or in musty corners of second-hand bookstores.**" After a life time of trying to destroy the Bible, Paine's dying words were a sobering tribute to the Bible's triumph: "***I would give worlds, if I had them, if the 'Age of Reason' had never been published. O Lord, help me! Christ, help me! Stay with me! It is hell to be left alone.***" [2]

Attacks continue from liberal theologians, worldly philosophers, modernists, humanists, rationalists, scientific skeptics, and every conceivable critic, but the Bible continues to live on.

(2) The Bible Has a Marvelous Unity

The Bible consists of sixty-six books, written in three different languages, with forty different writers, in three different continents, at least six different countries, written over a period of 1600 years. It covers hundreds of controversial subjects, and yet it has maintained a marvelous unity. You would expect any book that was produced from these circumstances to be a mass of conflicting statements and contradictions. Such is not the case with the Bible for it came from the mind of an all-knowing and all-powerful God.

"*Consider this: if you selected ten people living at the same time in history, living in the same basic geographical area, with the same basic educational background, speaking the same language, and you asked them to write independently on their conception of God, the result would be anything but a united testimony. It would not help if you asked them to write about man, woman, or human suffering, for it is the nature of human beings to differ on controversial subjects. However, the biblical writers ... have complete unity and harmony."* ³

For centuries the Bible has literally been picked apart, as its enemies search in vain for contradictions. One example that skeptics have called a contradiction has to do with the way Judas died. In Matt. 27:5 it states: *"Then he threw down the pieces of silver in the temple and departed, and went and hanged himself."* However, in Acts 1:18 we read: *"Now this man purchased a field with the wages of iniquity; and falling headlong, he burst open in the middle and all his entrails gushed out."* The Bible critics then rejoice, claiming that they have found a conflicting statement. This is not a contradiction at all! One Scripture merely supplements the other. Judas went out and hanged himself. At a later time he fell and burst open in the middle and his bowels gushed out. The rope, or that to which the rope was attached, may have broken. Perhaps the body began to decompose and fell. There is no contradiction here. One passage gives us information that is supplemented by another.

Many fine books have been written that detail alleged Bible contradictions along with reasonable explanations why they are not true contradictions.

(3) The Bible Has an Overwhelming Amount of Manuscript Evidence

"The manuscript evidence supporting the Bible's accuracy is overwhelming. There are over 5,500 Greek manuscripts of the New Testament, over 10,000 of the Latin Vulgate, and at least 9,300 other early versions. A combined total approaching nearly 25,000 manuscript copies or portions of the New Testament are in existence today." ⁴ Some portions of manuscripts date back to A. D. 120. Other fragments date between 150-200 years from the time of

the original composition. Two of the manuscripts that contain almost the entire New Testament are the Codex Vaticanus (A. D. 325) and the Codex Siniaticus (A. D. 350). These date within 250 years of the time of the original composition. This may seem like a long time span until we compare it to most ancient works. The earliest copy of Caesar's The Gallic Wars dates 1,000 years after it was written, and the first complete copy of the Odyssey by Homer 2,200 years after it was written.

The short interval of time between the copies and the writing of the original documents and the large number of manuscripts in existence give us unquestionable confidence in the reliability of the New Testament that we now have in our hands.

(4) The Bible Is Historically Accurate

Human history books have always required updating and correcting. This is not so with the Bible. For many years the skeptics made fun of the Bible's reference to the Hittite people (Gen. 23:10; 26:34), since no known works of secular history made reference to the Hittites. *"But suddenly, the archaeologist's spade uncovered at ancient Boghazkoy in modern Turkey an entire Hittite civilization!"* [5] Once again the critics of the Bible were wrong and the Bible was right.

Another example of the Bible proving to be historically correct is the case of Sargon, the king of Assyria. For many years, critics maintained that there never was a king of Assyria by that name. *"But then, in 1843, Paul Emil Botta, French Consul at Mosul in modern Iraq, in archaeological excavations on the east bank of the Tigris River, fourteen miles northeast of ancient Nineveh, discovered Khorsabad – the site of an elaborate, magnificent palace constructed by Sargon II in 706 B. C. The palace covered an area of twenty-five acres – a space larger than many contemporary cities in Palestine today."* ⁶ The Bible can be trusted for its historical accuracy.

(5) The Bible Prophecies Fulfilled

The Bible has proven itself to be true because it wrote history before it happened. Consider just the prophecies pertaining to Jesus. Fourteen hundred years before Jesus of Nazareth was born, his birth, life, and death, were foretold in detail. During the last twenty-four hours of the life of Jesus, at least twenty-five Old Testament prophecies were fulfilled.

There are 332 prophecies regarding Jesus alone that were fulfilled in the New Testament. Following is a list of just eight of those prophecies with their fulfillment. What would be the odds of one person literally fulfilling just those eight prophecies? Peter W. Stoner, chairman of the Mathematics and Astronomy Department at Pasadena City College until 1953 and chairman of the Science Division of Westmont College from 1953-57 applied the Law of Compound Probabilities to the area of prophetic fulfillment. The probability of one person fulfilling all eight prophecies would be 1 in 100,000,000,000,000,000! ⁷ Remember, this figure applies to the fulfillment of only eight out of 332!

1. He would be born in Bethlehem (Micah 5:2; Matt. 2:1).
2. He would be born of a virgin (Isa. 7:14; Matt. 1:18).
3. He would be betrayed for thirty pieces of silver (Zech. 11:12, 13; Matt. 26:15).
4. He would be smitten and spat upon (Isa. 50:6; Mark 14:65).
5. He would be crucified with thieves (Isa. 53:12; Matt. 27:38).
6. His hands and feet would be pierced (Ps. 22:16; John 20:27).
7. They would cast lots for His garments (Ps. 22:18; Mark 15:24).

8. He would be buried in a rich man's tomb (Isa. 53:9; Matthew 27:57-60).

If the number of fulfilled prophecies increased to 48, the odds of one person fulfilling all 48 would be 1 in 10^{x157}.[8] That is 10 with 157 zeros behind it! It has never happened in human history, except with the prophecies of Jesus. But, remember that there are not just forty-eight fulfilled prophecies, but there are 332! Even to try to contemplate one person fulfilling all 332 prophecies absolutely boggles the mind. And yet, Jesus did just that! If there were no other evidence for the inspiration of the Bible than its fulfilled prophecies, this alone would be sufficient. God is the author of the Bible.

(6) The Bible Is Geographically Accurate

Maps of the world must undergo constant change to remain accurate. Students cannot use world maps that are even ten years old because they have become obsolete. This is not so with the Bible. The Bible contains no geographical mistakes. The cities, towns, plains, deserts, hills and mountains mentioned in the Bible have been found exactly where the Bible said they would be.

Nineveh

There are places mentioned in the Bible that unbelieving scholars have even denied existed. One illustration is the case of Nineveh. The Old Testament book of Jonah declares: **"Now Nineveh was an exceedingly great city, a three-day journey in extent"** (Jonah 3:3). The scoffers once said, There is no such place as Nineveh and never has been. Furthermore, if there had been such a city, the idea of it being so large that it would take three days to cross it is pure nonsense. They are not laughing and scoffing anymore. After being under the dust for 2500 years, the shovels of archeologists uncovered the ancient city of Nineveh. It was there all the time just as the Bible stated. In regard to its size, they found that the distance from one suburb, through the city proper, and across the suburb on the other side was thirty miles. One day's journey when there were women and children in the party was ten miles. Therefore, the city of Nineveh was three days journey across.

Jerusalem and Jericho

Those who would discredit the Bible often point out an apparent mistake in geography because the Bible says that travelers went *"up"* to Jerusalem and *"down"* to Jericho. They show on the map that Jerusalem is south and Jericho is north and, therefore, they say, the Bible is wrong. No, the Bible is absolutely correct. Those who have traveled from Jerusalem to Jericho know that you descend in elevation, or go *"down"* to Jericho. When you travel from Jericho to Jerusalem, you rise in elevation, or go *"up"* to Jerusalem. The Bible makes no geographical mistakes.

(7) The Bible Contains No Scientific Mistakes

The Bible was never intended to be a textbook on science, but when it speaks in any area of science it speaks with accuracy. Modern science changes rapidly, but the Bible remains steadfast and accurate. If a student were studying some technical science from a text that was copyrighted twenty years earlier, that student would be hopelessly behind. In contrast, the Bible is a book that is never out of date. It was completed over 1900 years ago and yet it is as modern as today's newspaper.

Life is in the Blood

The Bible contains scientific information that was not discovered by scientists until hundreds of years later. In A. D. 1615 the discovery was made by Harvy concerning the circulation of the blood and that the life principle was in the blood. Lev. 17:11, written about 1400 B. C., states, *"The life of the flesh is in the blood."* By inspiration Moses declared something that was not "discovered" by scientists until 3,000 years later!

The Shape of the Earth

"As to the shape of the earth, Anaximenes said it is like a table, and Leucippus said it is like a drum. An ancient Persian map shows a flat world with a row of mountains around the edges. The flatness of the earth was generally believed until the sixteenth century after Christ." [9] But, in Proverbs 8:27, written about 1000 B. C., we read: *"He drew a circle on the face of the deep."* Then, look at Isaiah 40:22, written about 800 B. C.: *"It is he who sits above the circle of the earth."* How did Isaiah know that the earth was a spheroid 2500 years before science discovered it to be so? The answer is obvious. God wrote the Bible!

Foundation of the Earth

Until the early sixteenth century, scientists believed and taught that the earth rested on a solid foundation. Some believed that pillars of rock supported it. Among other ideas, some believed that it rested on a tortoise. It was not until the time of Galileo that people believed that the gigantic tonnage of the earth was actually unsupported. In Job 26:7 this very truth was declared 3000 years before Galileo: *"He stretches out the north over empty space; he hangs the earth on nothing."* The statement that Job made was most daring. Imagine the reaction of early readers of this announcement! Who revealed this truth to him? The answer is all too obvious. God revealed it to him!

(8) The Bible's Brevity and Restraint

The Bible was written for a special purpose, to convey God's will to man. It is placed in a unique class for many reasons, not the least of which is the brevity with which the Bible story is told. The purpose of the Bible was certainly not to satisfy human curiosity. If so, the result would have been totally different. The story of the creation of the universe is vividly told in only thirty-four verses. Twenty-five hundred years of man's history are told in fifty chapters of one book. The account of the baptism of Jesus was related in only five verses. The stilling of the sea took only five verses. The transfiguration of Jesus is told in only eight verses. Jesus' ministry of 1200 days is condensed to events of thirty-four days. In one chapter Stephen sets forth nearly 2,000 years of history. The death of the first apostle took only eleven words to describe.

If the inspired writers had been allowed to give us all the details of just those events mentioned, we certainly would not be able to carry about the completely revealed Word of God in one hand! If the writers would have been given a free hand to tell all that could be told, large buildings would be required to house the Word. Amazingly, we have everything that we need to know from God all wrapped up in one single volume. Its restraint and brevity point to God as the author.

(9) The Bible's Influence

The high moral standards of the Bible point to a source far above sinful humanity. No other book has had such an influence for good, as the Bible. What honest and sincere person has ever read the Bible, and did not become a better person for it? Because of the Bible's tremendous influence for good, the Christian is given additional confidence that it is God's revelation to man.

"Did you ever hear a man say, 'I used to steal, lie, drink, swindle, abuse my family, gamble, break up homes, beat my debts, and was an immoral citizen, but I was finally induced to read some books on infidelity, atheism and doubt, and now I go to church, treat my family decently, pay my debts, live a moral life, try to be a good neighbor and a good citizen as the result of the influence these books had on me?' No, and you never will for the Bible is the only book that has such an influence on men." [10] As long as the Bible has such an influence on man, the Christian can hold up the Bible and declare with confidence, "This is from God!"

(10) The Bible's Impartiality

The impartial way that the Bible describes its principal characters points to a higher authorship than mere human beings. Ordinarily, when a biography is written it emphasizes the good attributes of its character and minimizes the faults. Sometimes, if the purpose of the writing is to make the subject look especially bad, only the defects are emphasized. The Bible is amazingly objective, in that it just states the facts about a person, both good and bad. The intent appears not to condemn or to condone, but to relate factual information.

For example, the writer of Genesis records that Noah was a just and perfect man, but later it also records that he got drunk. David was a man after God's own heart, but he committed adultery with a woman, and had her husband killed. The writers tell us of the great faith of Abraham, but they also tell us how he lied. We are told of Peter's strength in declaring his allegiance to Jesus and then of his weakness when he denied Jesus three times.

The Biblical writers were ideal historians, catering to no one, and writing as if they had no favorites. The Bible reader cannot help but be impressed with the impartial way that each character is portrayed. Indeed, God directed the minds and hands of those who wrote the Bible.

Conclusion

Among the unique and admirable qualities of the Bible are: (1) Its indestructibility, (2) It does not contradict itself, (3) It has an overwhelming number of manuscripts to support it, (4) It is historically accurate, (5) Its prophecies have been fulfilled, (6) It is geographically correct, (7) It contains no scientific errors, (8) It is written with amazing brevity and restraint, (9) It has influenced untold numbers of people for good, (10) All characters are presented impartially.

Some purely human books may have one or two of these superior attributes, but there is only one book that has all ten, and that is the Bible. The supporting evidence concerning the Bible's divine authorship, accuracy, and trustworthiness is overwhelming. The sheer weight of evidence should lead the sincere skeptic to the inevitable conclusion that the Bible is the Word of God.

The Anvil

Last eve I paused beside a blacksmith's door,
And heard the anvil ring the vesper chime;
Then, looking in, I saw upon the floor,
Old hammers, worn with beating years of time.

"How many anvils have you had," said I,
"To wear and batter all these hammers so?"
"Just one," said he, and then with a twinkling eye,
"The anvil wears the hammers out, you know."

"And so," I thought, "the anvil of God's word
For ages skeptic blows have beat upon,
Yet, though the noise of falling blows was heard,
The anvil is unharmed, the hammers gone."

Footnotes

1. William R. Kimball, The Book of Books, College Press, Joplin, MO, 1978, p. 32
2. Kimball, p. 33
3. Josh McDowell, Reasons Skeptics Should Consider Christianity, Here's Life Pub., Inc., San Bernardino, CA, p. 79
4. McDowell, p. 116
5. Dave Miller, Piloting the Strait, Sain Pub. Co., Pulaski, TN, 1996, p. 440
6. Miller, p. 440
7. Kimball, pp. 62-65
8. Kimball, p. 66
9. Hugo McCord, From Heaven or From Men? Firm Foundation Pub. Co, Austin, TX, 1964, p. 33
10. George Dehoff, Why We Believe the Bible, Dehoff Pub., Murfreesboro, TN, 1956, p. 64

CHAPTER 8
WHY SHOULD I BELIEVE IN JESUS AS THE SON OF GOD?

Almost two thousand years ago one called Jesus was born in a small village to parents of no fame or earthly wealth. At the age of thirty he began his public ministry. At the age of thirty-three he was put through the mockery of a trial and was put to death. Since that time those who believe in him have boldly proclaimed that he was the Christ, the very Son of God.

Others have denied these claims and have called Jesus a myth, an impostor, or a fraud. Those who believe in Jesus need not shrink back in fear when confronted with such denials, for there are many solid reasons on which we can base our faith in the deity of Jesus.

In this chapter we will consider some of those reasons which should give us confidence to say as did Peter, that Jesus is *"the Christ, the Son of the living God"* Matthew 16:16 (NKJV). Jesus was bold in his claim of being the Son of God. *"Who, being in the form of God, did not consider it robbery to be equal with God, but made Himself of no reputation, taking the form of a bondservant, and coming in the likeness of men"* (Philippians 2:6-7).

Jesus claimed to have existed with the Father before the creation of the world, *"And now, O Father, glorify Me together with Yourself, with the glory which I had with You before the world was"* (John 17:5). He further claimed to have participated with the Father in the creation of all things, *"In the beginning was the Word, and the Word was with God, and the Word was God. He was in the beginning with God. All things were made through Him, and without Him nothing was made that was made."* (John 1:1-3). He further said that he was the Way, the Truth, and the Life and the only access to God the Father (John 14:6).

The Foundation of the Church

When Jesus asked Peter *"Who do you say that I am?"* Peter answered by saying, *"You are the Christ, the Son of the living God."* Jesus responded by saying, *"Upon this rock I will build My church"* (Matt. 16:18). The *"rock"* was the fact of the divinity of Jesus, that He was the Son of God. Upon that bedrock of truth rests the church, all that we stand for religiously, and our very hope for eternity. All the claims of Christianity rest upon this one thesis, that Jesus Christ is the Son of God.

You Can't Have It Both Ways

If the modernists are right and Jesus was the illegitimate son of Joseph and Mary, our faith is in vain, our hope in vain, and we are a people to be pitied. It is amazing that modernists and liberals, who are found in ample supply in many denominations, deny the deity of Jesus, deny His virgin birth, deny His resurrection from the dead, and still claim to be Christians. You can't have it both ways. Jesus is everything that He claimed to be or He is the greatest fraud that the world has ever known. If He were not the Son of God, then Jesus fooled more people and is the author of more false hope than any man who ever lived on the face of the earth.

Couldn't Jesus Be Just a Good Man, and Not the Son of God?

It is inconsistent that philosophers speak of Jesus as a philosopher and a good man, but deny that He is the Son of God. If He deceived as many people as some claim that He has, if He has led untold numbers astray, if He has fooled and deluded the masses, if He has lied and has given false hope to those who trusted Him, how can He be called good?

On the other hand, if He is the Son of God, then He is the gift from Heaven and the hope for all ages. With confidence we can believe that Jesus is everything that He claimed to be, the Christ, the promised Messiah, the son of the living God. Please consider the following seven (7) reasons to believe in Jesus as God's Son.

Reason Number One: He Was a True Historical Person

It is bewildering that a number of reasonably well educated people actually are not convinced that Jesus ever actually lived. They think of Him as a myth created in the minds of ignorant people. This is amazing in light of the evidence that verifies that He was a real historical figure. However, even honest people can have occasional doubts, and so it is good to remind ourselves of these facts.

Historians Included Jesus

In **"THE BIBLE AS HISTORY"** by Werner Keller, the writer quotes from a Roman historian named Tacitus. He mentions Jesus specifically in his writing called **"ANNALS"** while explaining the origin of the word **"Christians."** He said, *"Christ, from whom they derive their name, was condemned to death by the procurator*

Pontius Pilate in the reign of the Emperor Tiberius."

While a number of such historical references could be cited, we mention only one more. The Jewish historian, Flavius Josephus, never accepted Christianity. He was about thirty years younger than Jesus. In *"THE LIFE AND WORKS OF FLAVIUS JOSEPHUS"* P. 535, he wrote, *"Now there was about this time Jesus, a wise man, if it be lawful to call him a man."* As a non-believer, Josephus had no reason to invent a fictitious character, or to participate in some kind of conspiracy to make people believe in a myth. He was simply a historian reporting the facts. The existence of Jesus in history is a fact.

The Writers of the Gospels Attest to the Reality of Jesus in History

One might react by saying that Matthew, Mark, Luke, and John could hardly be credible witnesses since they were believers in Jesus. Our first response would be, *"Why would they believe in a non-existent person?"* The fact that they believed in Him and followed Him adds even greater believability to their accounts.

Contemporaries of Jesus

A very important consideration is the fact that these four men who wrote about Jesus were His contemporaries. The importance of this can hardly be overstated. Many of those living in the first century who read what Matthew, Mark, Luke, and John wrote were also contemporaries of Jesus. Some were even His neighbors. They could remember the events about which these men wrote. They could compare what they read with their own memories and experiences. These four men simply could not get away with reporting things that were not correct or events that had never happened.

They Wrote in Detail

When these men wrote about Jesus they included detail after detail that could be checked. They gave information in such a manner that the reader could easily go to the very place where an incident happened and talk with people who had been present when it occurred. They could even go to Nazareth and talk to the family of Jesus. If one were writing about a non-existent person he would refrain from writing anything that could be checked out. He would be vague and never include dates, places, events or names as the writers of the gospels did. These men wrote in such a manner that they seemed to invite the reader to investigate the reports.

What They Wrote about Him

From reading the four accounts of the Gospels, we know many things about Jesus. We know who He was, where He walked, where He slept, where He ate, who His friends were, who His enemies were, what made Him angry, what made Him happy, and what made Him sad. We know His earthly father's name, His grandfather's name, and His great-grandfather's name. In fact, we have His genealogy traced all the way back to Adam (Luke 3:23-28). Can you imagine anyone trying to give the family background of a non-existent person, one that could easily be checked?

The person who argues that Jesus never really lived either denies the facts or is not familiar with them.

Reason Number Two:
The Prophecies Fulfilled by Christ

One of the primary evidences of the deity of Jesus involves His fulfillment of a great number of minutely detailed prophecies that were given hundreds of years before His birth.

There are over 300 prophecies in the Old Testament that directly relate to the birth, life, ministry, death, and resurrection of Christ. To have these fulfilled by one man could not be merely chance or coincidence. The only explanation that will suffice is that the prophecies were given by the inspiration of God and fulfilled by Jesus. God gave these prophecies so that the one who fulfilled them could prove to the honest observer that He was from God.

Much of the Biography of Jesus Was Written before He Was Born

Before Jesus was born, the place of His birth was foretold as being Bethlehem (Micah 5:2). The amazing prophecy was made in Isaiah 7:14 that He would be born of a virgin. His forerunner, John the Baptist, was announced in advance by Malachi (Mal. 3:1). Hundreds of years before Jesus was born, Isaiah prophesied about His birth, character, ministry, and His death (Isaiah 53). His triumphant entry into Jerusalem was foretold by Zechariah (Zech. 9:9). His resurrection was prophesied in Psalms 16:10. The church that Jesus established was prophesied in Daniel 2:44.

It is astounding to learn that so much of Jesus' life on earth was foretold in such detail hundreds of years before He was born. These prophecies and their fulfillment demonstrate that Christ did come from God. With prophecy after prophecy, God announced to mankind that His Son was coming. He then saw to it that these prophecies were fulfilled. In so doing, God authenticated that Jesus was whom He claimed to be, the Son of God.

Reason Number Three:
The Nature of His Character

Even non-Christian historians admit that Jesus of Nazareth was the greatest man who ever lived. H.G. Wells said of Jesus, *"When I was asked which single individual has left the most permanent impression on the world, the manner of the questioner almost carried the implication that it was Jesus of Nazareth. I agreed."* (The Three Greatest Men of History, Readers Digest, May 1935) Very few historians would disagree with that conclusion.

No man could justly find fault with His life. He was humble, forgiving, patient, and morally pure. No man ever lived such a holy life as did Jesus. He exerted such tremendous power and influence over the lives of others that no one else in history can rightfully be compared to Him. This is exactly the kind of impact that we would expect God's Son to have.

Evidence Number Four: His Masterful Teaching

Like His life, the teachings of Jesus are totally unique. Each time that Jesus addressed an individual or a crowd, His words were perfect, powerful, and penetrating. He confounded His enemies and amazed His followers. His illustrations were natural and provided windows for His lessons.

The Sermon on the Mount

Probably the most familiar example of His unique teaching is found in the Sermon on the Mount. It is not an exaggeration to say that this is the greatest statement of moral and religious principles ever recorded. The words that Jesus uttered on that hillside some 2,000 years ago have been studied microscopically. Thousands of books and commentaries have been written on that single sermon. And yet, man has not exhausted the truths contained therein. Those words have never gone out of date, nor have they lost their power to transform the lives of men. When we pause to consider this single soul stirring message of Jesus, recorded in Matthew chapters 5-7, we are forced to say with Nicodemus, **"Rabbi, we know that You are a teacher come from God"** (John 3:2).

Evidence Number Five:
His Miracles Testify of His Deity

After Nicodemus heard Jesus speak, he declared Him to be a teacher from God. When he considered the miracles that Jesus did, he further declared **"No one can do these signs that you do unless God is with him"** (John 3:2). Indeed, the signs and miracles which Jesus performed constitute undeniable proof that He is the Christ, the Son of the living God. Just consider the magnificent miracles that Jesus did and then explain how He could do these things if He were not divine. Obviously, one could not.

1. He walked on the water (John 6:15-21).
2. He stilled the storm on the Sea of Galilee (Matt. 8:23-27).
3. Jesus made the blind to see (Matt. 9:27-31).
4. He cleansed the leper (Luke 5:12-14).
5. He made the deaf to hear and the dumb to speak (Mark 7:31-37).
6. Jesus removed the demon which possessed a boy (Luke 9:44).
7. He fed about 5,000 people by the miraculous multiplication of a few loaves and fishes (John 6:10-12).
8. On three occasions He even raised the dead to life again (Luke 7, Luke 8, John 11).

Skeptics will argue that these are simply made-up stories, concocted by fanatical disciples, intent on convincing people that Jesus was a divine person. However, we must remember that Matthew, Mark, Luke, and John wrote their accounts not many years after these events took place. This was not the case that sometimes happens when an event takes place and several hundred years pass before the incident is recorded. When the writers recorded the miracles of Jesus there were many who were still alive who were eyewitness of those miracles.

His Miracles Were Done in Public

Jesus did not perform His miracles in private and then have His disciples declare them publicly. He performed them in a variety of places, many times in cities, surrounded by crowds of people. There was nothing hidden about them. Such complete openness with which His miracles took place invited investigation. He performed them in the presence of unbelieving critics and put them to silence with His display of divine power.

There was No Evidence to Contradict

If the enemies of Jesus could have submitted any evidence to contradict Christ's claim to supernatural power, they would have done so, and the matter would have been settled for all time. The fact is, that they could not produce one single bit of evidence showing that what Jesus did was by slight-of-hand or trickery.

When Judas betrayed Jesus, what greater harm could he have done to Jesus than to show His enemies that His miracles were fraudulent, and then tell them how He did it? Judas could not do this, for the miracles of Jesus were authentic. The only thing that he could do was to tell His enemies where Jesus was praying. All the evidence is in favor of the truthfulness of the New Testament account of the miraculous works of Christ. The unbeliever has nothing but his unbelief with which to challenge the record. He has no facts to contradict.

Evidence Number Six: The Events Surrounding His Death

The events surrounding the death of Jesus were unlike any that had ever occurred before. When Jesus died, darkness fell over the whole land (Luke 23:44). The veil of the temple was torn in two from top to bottom (Matt. 27:51). The earth shook (v. 51). The rocks were split (v. 51). Tombs were opened and the dead bodies of believers were raised to life again (v. 52).

The Roman centurion saw all the things that attended the death of Christ and cried out *"Truly this was the Son of God"* (v. 54). Jesus even predicted the time and place that He would be put to death. *"From that time Jesus began to show to His disciples that He must go to Jerusalem, and suffer many things from the elders and chief priests and scribes, and be killed, and be raised the third day"* (Matt. 16:21). These events were experienced by people who lived to read about them in the writings of Matthew, Mark, Luke, and John, and yet not a single person wrote a single line denying the accuracy of those reports.

Evidence Number Seven: The Resurrection of Jesus

The bodily resurrection of Jesus is crucial to Christ's claim of being God's Son. The whole Christian system rests or falls on the resurrection. If this doctrine stands the test of investigation, the whole of the Christian religion may be accepted without reservation. On the other hand, if it doesn't stand the test, the Christian religion is of no value than the religions of Buddha or Mohammed.

The Resurrection Was Foretold

The doctrine of the resurrection of Jesus did not develop accidentally, nor did the devoted disciples of Jesus invent the doctrine and popularize it among certain uneducated and superstitious classes of people. The resurrection of Jesus was foretold hundreds of years before it happened (Ps. 16:10).

Jesus repeatedly made reference to His death and resurrection from the dead during the years of His public ministry. *"Destroy this temple and in three days I will raise it up, but He was speaking of the temple of His body"* (John 2:19, 21).

The early disciples claimed that Jesus did indeed rise from the dead. Preaching in the city of Jerusalem on the first Pentecost following the crucifixion of Christ, Peter said that God raised Jesus from the dead in fulfillment of prophecies given through David, and he, Peter, claimed to be a witness of the resurrection (Acts 2). Still, we are left with the question of proof. What evidence can be presented in favor of the contention that Jesus really did rise from the dead on the Sunday morning following His death? To prove the resurrection is to prove the divinity of Jesus.

Please consider the following Six Points of Evidence that Jesus was resurrected from the grave.

Resurrection Evidence Number One: The Empty Tomb

Jesus died on Friday afternoon. He was buried in the tomb of Joseph of Arimathea which was located in a garden near the place of crucifixion (John 19:41). The burial took place under the supervision of men who were assigned by Pilate to make sure the disciples could not take the body and claim that He was resurrected. After the burial and sealing of the tomb, the guard was posted to keep watch over the place. Extra precaution was no doubt taken since Jesus said in advance that He would rise.

One fact that has not been disputed by even the most bitter enemies of Christianity is that the TOMB WAS EMPTY on the following Sunday morning. The seal had been set. The guard was there. But, Jesus was gone! Jesus walked out of that tomb on Sunday morning.

Resurrection Evidence Number Two: The Orderly Condition inside the Tomb

The tomb was empty, but the linen body wrappings were still there. The face cloth had been rolled up and placed by itself (John 20:6-7). Josh McDowell suggested that the observers of the empty tomb probably saw the body wrappings still in the form of a body like an empty caterpillar's cocoon. The preparation of the body for burial included the wrapping of the body with gauze-like strips (John 19:40).

It is unreasonable and even ridiculous to suggest that grave robbers took the body. In order for this to have happened, the following would have had to occur.

1. Under penalty of death they would have to break the Roman seal.
2. Under the very noses of the Roman guards they would have had to roll the stone away and break into the tomb without being seen or heard.
3. Inside the tomb they would have had to take the time to unwrap the body of Jesus and put everything neatly in order.

Then they would have had to leave the tomb, carrying the body of Jesus without being seen by the guards. The idea is absurd! The body was not stolen!

Resurrection Evidence Number Three: The Testimony of Witnesses Who Saw Jesus Alive after His Crucifixion

After Jesus had been killed, buried, and resurrected, He appeared to different individuals or groups of people on ten different occasions:

1. Jesus appeared to Mary Magdalene at the tomb (John 20:11-18).
2. He appeared to Simon Peter (Luke 24:34).
3. He appeared to two disciples on the road to Emmaus (Luke 24:13-35).
4. He appeared to ten of the apostles in a private room with Thomas absent (John 20:19-25).
5. He appeared to the apostles with Thomas present (John 20:26-29).
6. He appeared to a number of disciples as they were fishing (John 21:1-20).
7. He appeared to 500 brethren at one time (I Corinthians 15:6).
8. He appeared to James (I Corinthians 15:7).
9. He appeared to all the apostles at Jerusalem just before ascending from the Mount of Olives (Luke 24:50-52).
10. He appeared to Saul of Tarsus on the road to Damascus (I Corinthians 15:8, Acts 9:5).

If one witness of good reputation tells us something, we are inclined to believe him. If two witnesses agree, the story is very convincing, but if more than 500 witnesses have the same story to tell, the evidence becomes overwhelming. More than 500 witnesses, on 10 different occasions saw Jesus alive after He had been seen dead. The witnesses saw Him with their eyes, touched Him with their hands, ate with Him, talked with Him, walked with Him. Upon physical examination, Thomas was moved to say, **"My Lord and my God"** (John 20:28).

Resurrection Evidence Number Four: The Lives of the Disciples after the Resurrection

Many of the early disciples spent their whole lives preaching the resurrected Christ. They did so at their own peril. Some were beaten, driven out of cities, imprisoned, tortured, or even put to death. They endured all these things rather than deny the resurrected Christ. Does anyone honestly believe that this group of men could have been so motivated by a story, which they knew to be a lie? The idea is absurd! They were willing to die for their faith because they knew beyond a shadow of a doubt that Jesus rose from the grave.

Resurrection Evidence Number Five: The Silence of the World as to the Whereabouts of the Body

Seven weeks after the resurrection, Peter stood up on the day of Pentecost and preached the resurrection of Christ as an absolute fact. What would have been more devastating to his message than for the Jews to have produced the body of Jesus? Had they been able to do so, they would have done it. In doing so, the whole of Christianity would have been destroyed! (I Corinthians 15:17). Their silence is as loud as the speaking of Christians who witnessed the resurrection.

Resurrection Evidence Number Six: There was No Contradictory Evidence

Nobody said, *"I was there too. I know the story is a fake. I can tell you exactly how they fooled you."* There was no contradictory evidence then and there is none now. Please remember this very important fact: the claim that Jesus had risen from the dead was first published in the very city where it happened. And, no one was able to prove that it didn't happen! The apostles didn't run off to some far off part of the world to tell about the resurrection. They told about it in the city where it happened. The tomb could be examined. Witnesses could be questioned. Every fact could be investigated.

The enemies of Christianity desperately wanted to put a stop to the resurrection message, but, because of the facts, they were powerless to do so. The only fair and reasonable conclusion is that the disciples were telling the truth. Jesus really did walk out of that tomb alive!

CHAPTER 9
WHY SHOULD I BELIEVE IN GOD?

Is there a God? In all of human existence there cannot be a more profound question. As we consider our very lives and all that we hold dear, we realize that everything is affected by the answer to this one question. On what basis can we conclude that there is a God? The atheist states that God must not exist since we cannot see Him or touch Him. While it is true that we cannot put God in a test tube, it does not follow that this disproves His existence. In this chapter we will briefly discuss eight reasons to believe in God.

Reason Number One:
The Inclination for Man to Be Religious

Man has a natural intuition of the existence of God. He is incurably religious. Wherever man has been found, in ancient times or modern times, this has been found to be a part of his nature. It really doesn't matter if he is rich or poor, educated or uneducated, he seeks a higher being. The Psalmist declared, *"As the deer pants for the water brooks, so pants my soul for You, O God. My soul thirsts for God, for the living God"* (Psalms 42:1-2).

Anthropological research has indicated there is a universal belief in God among the most remote peoples today. *"Whether by means of intellect or spirit, the fact is that man has almost universally recognized a greater all-encompassing intelligence and order in the universe than could possibly be conceived from chance, haphazard events involving inanimate, unguided matter. That man universally accepts the need of extrapolation beyond his own intellect is in itself strong evidence for a superior Intelligence."* [1]

While this intuition is universally common to man, it is totally absent from lower animals. There is something about the way that we human beings are made that causes us to know that we, as well as the universe around us, are products from God.

Reason Number Two: Cause and Effect

No effect can be produced without a cause. We have no difficulty in accepting the fact that where a house exists there had to be those who caused that house to come into existence. Where there is an automobile there must have been a manufacturer. Where there is a world there must have been a Cause. Where there is a creation, there must have been a Creator.

A cause is needed to explain the source of inanimate things such as the sun, moon, planets and stars. If something exists it means that there was a Cause to make them exist. "Nothing comes from nothing." It is unreasonable to accept the idea that a house happened without a cause. Seen or unseen, someone built the house. It is unreasonable to accept the idea that the universe just happened without a Cause, without a Creator.

Consider the Human Mind

When one considers the human mind, the fact that a Cause is necessary to explain this is even more apparent. It is totally unreasonable and unacceptable that the mind of man came from unthinking matter. The fact that man can think demands a Creator who can think. The source of the mind of man is a greater Mind. The fact that man can reason demands a Rational Being behind it. The fact that we can know demands a greater One who knows.

Consider the Telescope

Did the telescope make itself? No one in his right mind would answer that it did. If the telescope did not make itself, then how could the human eye have made itself? If there is an intelligent cause behind the system that delivers water to every part of a city, then how can anyone deny that there was a Cause behind the system of veins and arteries that delivers blood to every part of the body?

The Watchmaker

I look at my watch and know that it had an intelligent maker. Although I have never seen that watchmaker, I have complete confidence that he existed. I have seen his handiwork. He had the power and intelligence to bring my watch into existence. I would be very foolish to take the position that the watchmaker never existed because I have never seen him, although I have seen the work of his hands. In like manner, we have seen the handiwork of God, and we can know that He was the Cause.

Reason Number Three: Arrangement

A third major reason to believe in God is the evidence seen in the arrangement of the universe and all that was created. Such intricate arrangement demands an intelligent Arranger. When one opens a can of alphabet soup and pours it out, he would not expect the letters to form the Declaration of Independence. No one can conceive of such a thing *"just happening."* For those letters to form words, sentences, and paragraphs, there must not only be a maker of the letters, but there must also be a planner and an arranger as well.

Arrangement of the Body

"Just as a poem assumes the existence of a poet, and a musical composition assumes a composer, so the regular selection and combination of exactly sixty-four chemical elements to form the human body assumes a great Chemist." [2] The human body is an absolutely amazing mechanism, composed of a skeletal system, a nervous system, a muscular system, a respiratory system, a circulatory system, a digestive system, a reproductive system, a system of touch, hearing, smelling, feeling, and seeing. Each system is amazing in its own right by design and function. But, when we add the fact that all of these systems work together in perfect harmony, we must conclude that there had to be an Intelligent Designer. To conclude that all of this just happened accidentally is beyond the realm of possibility.

The Heavens

One can gaze into the heavens and behold the work of an Almighty Designer, the moon, the stars and planets all functioning with magnificent preciseness. Well did the Psalmist state, *"The heavens declare the glory of God; and the firmament shows his handiwork"* (Psalms 19:1). What person could look into the starlit sky of the night and honestly conclude that such majesty just happened by itself. *"When I consider Your heavens, the* work of Your fingers, the moon and the stars, which You have ordained, what is man that You are mindful of him...?" (Psalms 8:3-4).

Halley's Comet

In 1682 Edmund Halley, an English astronomer identified a particular comet. He had such faith in the order and preciseness of the heavenly bodies that he predicted by mathematical calculation that the same comet would reappear every seventy-six years. Halley died in 1742, but in 1758 Halley's Comet indeed did appear right on schedule, and continued to reappear in its regular orbit in 1834, 1910, and 1986. Such regularity demands a Regulator.

Law and Order

Elmer W. Maurer, research chemist, stated that the scientific method depends upon the orderliness of the universe. *"It is impossible for me to conceive the law and order of the universe as being the result of pure chance. The odds are simply too great. Law, order and intelligence go hand in hand. Also, as a scientist I believe that God has permanent control of His world. He sees to it that there is fixedness and permanence in Nature's laws. When I step into my laboratory I know that the laws that hold true today will hold true tomorrow, and the next day, and as long as the universe exists... I have found nothing in natural science, in chemistry, that conflicts with the Bible. Nor do I find anything in the Bible that conflicts with science. The God of Genesis, I am convinced, is the sole answer to both the 'genesis' and the unfailing, detailed management of the world."* [3]

Reason Number Four: Design

"If the universe exhibits design, there must be a great Designer; if it shows thought, there must be a great Thinker; if it is run by the laws of nature, there must be a great Lawgiver; if it operates with mathematical precision, there must be a great Mathematician; if the universe gives us important chemical combinations, there must be a great Chemist. Thomas A. Edison said that the universe is such an engineering feat, 'There must be a Great Engineer.' From these conclusions there is no escape. God exists." 4

A Great Designer

The human body is an excellent example of intentional design. The feet are attached to the ankles to allow for walking. The fingers are attached to the hand to make it possible to grip and hold. The knees are made so that running is possible. As we look at each member of our body we see the work of a Great Designer.

Consider the Human Eye

Perhaps the greatest marvel of design of all in the human body is the eye. The elements of the eye are arranged to form an optic nerve, retina, lens, pupil, iris, and cornea. Somehow all of these come together to give us something that we call sight. "Even Darwin himself in a chapter from his *The Origins of Species* titled Difficulties with the Theory states: 'To suppose that the eye, with so many parts all working together...could have formed by natural selection, seems, I freely confess, absurd in *the highest degree."* [5] A Source capable of producing the marvel of sight cannot Himself be blind.

A Perfect World

The earth itself is important evidence of meticulous design. Dr. A. Cressy Morrison, former president of the New York State Academy of Science made this observation: *"We have found that the world is in the right place, that the crust is adjusted to within 10 feet, and that if the ocean were a few feet deeper we would have no oxygen or vegetation. We have found that the earth rotates in twenty-four hours and that were this revolution delayed, life would be impossible. If the speed of the earth around the sun were increased or decreased materially, this history of life, if any, would be entirely different. We find that the sun is the one among thousands which could make our sort of life possible on earth, its size, density, temperature and the character of its rays all must be right, and are right. We find that the gases of the atmosphere are adjusted to each other and that a very slight change would be fatal..."* [6] Who placed the earth and the heavens in exactly the right location? Who tilted the earth on its axis to insure the seasons? Who designed such perfection? The answer is a Perfect Designer, God.

Reason Number Five:
The Moral Law Within

Within human beings there is a law of right and wrong. The standards may vary, but the fact remains that a sense of right and wrong is common to all. Even among heathen people there is something that causes them to reject certain acts of behavior as unacceptable. This moral sense within man is not merely the result of cultural norms or cultural standards. It is an inborn capacity to know right from wrong morally.

"That man has this capacity can hardly be explained unless there is a moral governor of the universe. It implies a moral creator, God. It is universally observed that human beings try to convince themselves that their actions are right and justifiable. They desire the approval of their consciences, as well as the approval of their fellowmen. Is it unreasonable to assume that the presence of a moral nature in man is an indication of a moral governor? Why should man be concerned with the demands of conscience if he is nothing more than a chance combination of atoms?"[7]

Those Who Have No Law

Paul recognized this inner sense of right and wrong when he wrote, *"For when Gentiles, who do not have the law, by nature do the things in the law, these, although not having the law, are a law to themselves, who show the work of the law written in their hearts, their conscience also bearing witness, and between themselves their thoughts accusing or else excusing them"* (Romans 2:14-15).

Conscience

If there is a moral law, there must then be a moral Lawgiver. The Bible tells us that man was made in the image of God. Man was created with a soul, but he also was given a conscience. In creation, man was distinguished from all other creatures.

"This moral image comes with us at birth regardless of our origins or nationality. One never hears a pet ask, 'Is this right or wrong?' or 'is this good or bad?' Such ideas are unique to human beings, and for human beings the moral image is not optional software. Yes, there is Somebody behind the universe. He is God who has mind, emotions, conscience and will, Himself a complete personality. These ingredients were given to us when He created us, and they included a moral law. He is intensely interested in right conduct – in fair play, unselfishness, courage, good faith, honesty and truthfulness." [8]

Reason Number Six:
Belief in God Is the Most Reasonable Explanation

Belief in God provides the simplest and most reasonable explanation for many important questions. "How did the universe come into existence?" *"How can such amazing order in the universe be explained?" "What is the meaning of life?" "Why does man have the desire for immortality?"* Belief in God answers all of these questions. Atheism answers none of them. *"If the right key is the one that fits the lock and opens the door, then theism (belief in God) is the right key, not atheism. Darwin's solution left him, he said, 'in an utterly hopeless muddle.'"* [9]

Atheism Is Not Reasonable

It is far more reasonable to believe in God than it is to accept Atheism. The Atheist claims to believe he has no creator. *"Before anyone can proclaim 'there is no God' he ought to have made extensive explorations in heaven and earth, in the material world and the spiritual world, in time and eternity. Before he can know there is no God he would himself have to become one – he would have to be omniscient or the one thing he did not know might be that God exists."* [10]

Mind or Matter?

It is reasonable to accept the premise that something has always existed. The earth exists. We exist. The universe exists. But, what is the origin of it all? Since *"something cannot come from nothing"* it logically follows that something was self-existent. Something always was. There are but two things in existence, mind and matter. The atheist wants us to believe that matter was that thing which always existed, but it is far more reasonable to accept the fact that mind (a living, intelligent, Divine Being) has existed from eternity, not matter.

Without question, mind is superior to matter. *"Mind is the knowing entity, while matter is the object known. Mind impresses, moves, and modifies matter. Matter is the servant and mind the master."* [11] The chemist is greater than his chemicals and the mind is greater than the body that it controls. The Atheist supposes that matter is eternal and it has created mind, intellect and life; but the believer in God contends that mind, Almighty God, has existed from all eternity and has created the material universe. Which position is more reasonable?

A Product of Sheer Chance?

Atheism maintains the unreasonable position that the universe is the product of sheer chance. One who will honestly and objectively look at the universe will see design demonstrated everywhere. This design demands a designer.

"The opposite of design is chance. No design, no plan, no action toward the realization of a plan, no intelligence, no God; then chance is the word and the conception, though the thing, chance itself, can not be proved to have even an existence. A glance at some of nature's works would seem to

make the absurdity of this supposition sufficiently evident. Is the eye, with all its nice and scientific adjustment, a work of chance? Is it a matter of chance that the human heart has its valves, arteries, veins and vital powers? Did chance create the human ear and its correlation with the vocal apparatus? Was it chance that gave the hand its powers and the brain its functions? Was it by chance that all these organs of the human body were brought together in the being called man?" [12]

Abundance of Evidence

The reasonable person will listen to evidence before making a decision in a matter before him. *"The questioning mind can find almost an unlimited number of reasons for believing in God. We decide other questions by the preponderance of evidence. Why not this one? Suggestive of the lines of proof which might be developed... intuitional, ontological, cosmological, geological, astronomical, physio-theological, psychological, historical, providential, and ethical. Yet, skeptics claim they cannot find any line of proof to indicate the existence of God! Shall we say they cannot or will not?"* [13]

When all is said and done, it is far more reasonable to believe in an Eternal God who in the beginning *"created the heavens and the earth,"* and then *"created man in His own image"* (Gen. 1:1, 27) than to conclude that it all just happened by chance.

Reason Number Seven: The Bible Declares God

The Bible is of supernatural origin. It has proven itself by an abundance of evidence to be from God. The Bible testifies that God exists. From beginning to end the existence of God is declared. *"In the beginning God created the heavens and the earth"* (Gen.

1:1). *"Let all the earth fear the Lord; let all the inhabitants of the world stand in awe of Him"* (Psalms 33:8). *"The Lord reigns; let the earth rejoice"* (Psalms 97:1). *"God, who made the world and everything in it, since He is Lord of heaven and earth, does not dwell in temples made with hands"* (Acts 17:24).

The Bible makes bold, unmistakable claims to inspiration. *"All Scripture is given by inspiration of God, and is profitable for doctrine, for reproof, for correction, for instruction in righteousness"* (2 Tim. 3:16).

Seven Lines of Evidence to Believe the Bible

The skeptic questions the divine origin of the Bible and its veracity, but rest assured, it will stand each test to which it is subjected. We will briefly notice seven lines of evidence that the Bible came from God.

1. <u>The Bible is indestructible:</u> It has weathered the test of time, being the most attacked book ever written. It has been attacked by so called *"higher critics"* who tried to teach the Bible out of existence, and by atheists who tried to laugh the Bible out of existence. They all failed. The Bible has been the subject of attacks from liberal theologians, worldly philosophers, modernists, humanists, rationalists, scientific skeptics, and every conceivable critic, but they have failed and the Bible continues to live on.

2. <u>The Bible Has Amazing Unity:</u> The Bible consists of sixty-six books, written in three different languages, with forty different writers, on three different continents, and in at least six different countries, written over a period of 1600 years. It covers hundreds of controversial subjects, and yet

it has maintained a marvelous unity. You would expect any book that was produced from these circumstances to be a mass of conflicting statements and contradictions. Such is not the case with the Bible for it came from the mind of an all-knowing and all-powerful God.

3. <u>Overwhelming Manuscript Evidence:</u> The manuscripts supporting the accuracy of the New Testament alone are overwhelming. *"There are over 5,500 Greek manuscripts of the New Testament, over 10,000 of the Latin Vulgate, and at least 9,300 other early versions. A combined total approaching nearly 25,000 manuscript copies or portions of the New Testament are in existence today."* [14] Some portions of manuscripts date back to AD 120. Other early fragments date between 150-200 years from the time of the original composition. Two of the manuscripts that contain almost the entire New Testament are the Codex Vaticanus (AD 325) and the Codex Siniaticus (AD 350). The short interval of time between the copies and the writing of the original documents, and the large number of manuscripts in existence give us unquestionable confidence that what we have in our hands is God's Word.

4. <u>Historically Accurate:</u> Human history books have always required updating and correcting. This is not so with the Bible. For many years the skeptics made fun of the Bible's reference to the Hittite people (Gen. 23:10; 26:34), since no known works of secular history made reference to the Hittites. *"But suddenly, the archaeologist's spade uncovered at ancient Boghazkoy in modern Turkey an entire Hittite civilization!"* [15] The Bible can be trusted for its historical accuracy.

5. <u>Prophecies Fulfilled:</u> The Bible has proven itself to be true because of fulfilled prophecies. History was written before it happened. Consider just the prophecies pertaining to Jesus. Fourteen hundred years before Jesus was born, His birth, life, and death were foretold in detail. During the last twenty-four hours of the life of Jesus, at least twenty-five Old Testament prophecies were fulfilled. These prophecies came from the mind of God. This absolutely could not have been possible with human beings.

6. <u>Geographically Accurate:</u> Maps of the world must undergo constant change to remain accurate. Students cannot use world maps that are even ten years old because they have become obsolete. In contrast, the Bible can be counted upon to be accurate geographically. It contains no geographical mistakes. The cities, towns, plains, deserts, hills and mountains mentioned in the Bible have been found exactly where the Bible said they would be.

7. <u>No Scientific Mistakes:</u> The Bible was never intended to be a textbook on science, but when it speaks in any area of science it speaks with accuracy. Modern science changes rapidly, but the Bible remains steadfast and accurate. The Bible contains scientific information that was not discovered by scientists until hundreds of years later. For example, in AD 1615 the discovery was made by Harvy concerning the circulation of the blood and that the life principle was in the blood. Lev. 17:11, written about 1400 BC states, *"For the life of the flesh is in the blood."* By inspiration Moses declared something that was not discovered by scientists until 3,000 years later.

Until the sixteenth century, scientists believed and taught that the earth rested on a solid foundation. It was not until the time of Galileo that people believed that the earth was actually unsupported. In Job 26:7 this very truth was declared 3,000 years before Galileo: *"He stretches out the north over empty space; He hangs the earth on nothing."* Who revealed this "unknown" truth to Job? The answer must be that God revealed it to him!

The Bible is God's textbook. It has proven itself to be true and reliable. Since the Bible is true what it says about the existence of God must therefore be true.

Reason Number Eight: God Revealed Himself in Jesus

John declared of Jesus, *"And the Word became flesh and dwelt among us, and we beheld His glory, the glory as of the only begotten of the Father, full of grace and truth"* (John 1:14). Jesus came to earth to reveal the Father (John 1:18). Jesus was bold in his claim of being divine. In speaking of Christ, Paul said, *"Who being in the form of God, did not consider it robbery to be equal with God, but made Himself of no reputation, taking the form of a bondservant, and coming in the likeness of man"* (Phil. 2:6-7).

"One of the most defensible and utterly devastating arguments for the existence of God is the historical person and influence of Jesus of Nazareth. There is absolutely no way to explain Jesus apart from the fact that He came from God." [16] We can believe in God because we believe in Jesus who came from the Father. Let us consider just four evidences of the divinity of Jesus.

1. <u>A True Historical Character:</u> There should be no question among intelligent people that Jesus was a true historical character. Secular historians of the time of Jesus include Him in their writings. The Roman historian, Tacitus, mentions Jesus in his Annals while explaining the origin of the word "Christians." He said, *"Christ, from whom they derive their name, was condemned to death by the procurator Pontius Pilate in the reign of the Emperor Tiberius."* [17]

   The Jewish historian, Flavius Josephus, never accepted Christianity. He was about thirty years younger than Jesus. Josephus, when writing about events that took place under Pilate, said, *"Now there was about this time Jesus, a wise man, if it be lawful to call him a man, for he was a doer of wonderful works, a teacher of such men as had a veneration for truth. He drew over to Him both many of the Jews and many of the Gentiles: He was the Christ."* [18] As a non-believer, Josephus had no reason to invent a fictitious character, or to participate in some kind of conspiracy to make people believe in a myth. Without question, Jesus was a real person in history.

2. <u>Prophecies Were Fulfilled by Jesus:</u> One of the primary evidences of the deity of Jesus involves his fulfillment of a great number of minutely detailed prophecies which were given hundreds of years before his birth. There are over three hundred prophecies in the Old Testament which directly relate to the birth, life, ministry, death, and resurrection of Christ. To have these fulfilled by one man could not be merely chance or coincidence. The only explanation that will suffice is that the prophecies were given by the inspiration

of God and fulfilled by the Son of God. God gave those prophecies so that the one who fulfilled them could prove to the honest observer that he was from God.

3. <u>His Miracles Testify of his Deity:</u> Jesus showed that He was divine by walking on the water (John 6:15-21), stilling the storm of the sea (Matt. 8:23-27), making the blind to see (Matt. 9:27-31), cleansing the leper (Luke 5:12-14), healing the deaf and dumb (Mark 7:31-37), multiplying five loaves of bread and two fish to feed a multitude of about five thousand people (John 6:10-12), and even raising the dead to life again (Luke 7, Luke 8, John 11).

Skeptics will argue that these are simply made-up stories, designed to convince people that Jesus was a divine person. We must remember that Matthew, Mark, Luke, and John wrote their accounts not many years after these events took place. When these writers recorded the miracles of Jesus there were many still alive that were eyewitnesses of those miracles. Had the reports been untrue or misrepresented, it would have been very simple for those witnesses to deny them.

4. <u>The Resurrection of Jesus:</u> The bodily resurrection of Jesus is crucial to Christ's claim of being God's Son and therefore representing God. If this doctrine stands the test of investigation, then the whole of the Christian religion may be accepted without reservation. Some of the evidences that Jesus really did rise from the dead are as follows:

<u>(a) The Empty Tomb:</u> Jesus died on Friday afternoon and was buried in a tomb in a garden near where He was crucified

(John 19:41). The burial was supervised by men who were assigned by Pilate to make sure Christ's disciples would not take the body and claim that He was resurrected. After the burial and sealing of the tomb, the Roman guard was posted to keep watch. One fact that has not been disputed by even the most bitter of the enemies of Christianity is that the tomb was empty on the following Sunday morning. The guard had been set, but Jesus was gone.

(b) The Multitude of Witnesses: After Jesus had been killed, buried, and resurrected, He appeared to more than five hundred witnesses. These appearances took place on ten different occasions. If one witness of good reputation tells us something, we are inclined to believe him. If two witnesses agree, the story is very convincing, but if more than five hundred witnesses have the same story to tell, the evidence becomes overwhelming. Witnesses saw the resurrected Christ with their eyes, touched Him with their hands, ate with Him, talked with Him, and walked with Him.

(c) The Lives of His Disciples: Many of the early disciples spent their whole lives preaching the resurrected Christ. They did so at their own peril. They were beaten, driven out of cities, imprisoned, tortured, and even put to death. They endured all these things rather than deny the resurrected Christ. How could anyone honestly believe that this group of men could have been motivated in this way by a story that they knew to be a lie? The idea is absurd! They were willing to die for their faith because they knew beyond a shadow of a doubt that Jesus rose from the grave. He came from God!

(d) Where is the Body? Seven weeks after the resurrection, Peter stood up on the day of Pentecost and preached the resurrection of Christ as an absolute fact. What would have been more devastating to his message than for the Jews to have produced the body of Jesus. Had they been able to do so, the whole of Christianity would have been destroyed! Their silence is as loud as the testimony of Christians who witnessed the resurrection.

(e) No Contradictory Evidence: Nobody said, *"I was also there. I know the story is a hoax. I can tell you exactly how they fooled you."* There was no contradictory evidence then, and there is none now. The claim that Jesus had risen from the dead was first published in the very city where it happened. And yet, no one was able to offer any proof that the resurrection didn't happen! The tomb could be examined. Witnesses could be questioned. Every fact could be investigated. The resurrected Christ is proof that God exists.

Jesus testified of the existence of God. We can believe Him because He came from the Father. He has proven His divinity in countless ways.

Conclusion

As we examine the evidence of the existence of God, we are forced to the conclusion that it far easier to believe in God than it is not to believe. Ultimately, man must believe in God or Atheism. It makes more sense to believe in God. The Psalmist clearly identified the position of the unbeliever, *"The fool has said in his heart 'there is no God'"* (Psalms 14:1).

Faith in God is the logical conclusion. In our faith we need not waver or wonder. We can say with great confidence, *"In the beginning God created the heavens and the earth"* (Gen. 1:1). We can say with the Psalmist, *"The Lord reigns; let the earth rejoice"* (Psalms 97:1). We can be emboldened by Paul's observation, *"For since the creation of the world His invisible attributes are clearly seen, being understood by the things that are made, even His eternal power..."* (Rom. 1:20).

Footnotes

1. Batsell Barrett Baxter, I Believe Because..., Baker Bible House, Grand Rapids, Michigan, 1971, p. 41.
2. Hugo McCord, From Heaven or From Men?, Firm Foundation Pub. Co., Austin, Texas, 1964, p. 7
3. Baxter, pp. 62,63
4. George Dehoff, Why We Believe the Bible, Dehoff Pub., Murfreesboro, TN, 1956, pp. 20,21
5. Paul E. Little, Know Why You Believe, InterVarsity Press, Downers Grove, IL, 1988, p. 29
6. Baxter, p. 45
7. Little, p. 33
8. Baxter, p. 66
9. McCord, p. 11
10. Dehoff, p. 16
11. Harvey W. Everest, The Divine Demonstration, Christian Pub. Co., St. Louis, MO, 1884, p. 126
12. Everest, p. 137
13. Dehoff, pp. 23,24
14. Josh McDowell, Answers to Tough Questions, Here's Life Pub., Inc., San Bernardino, CA, 1980, p. 116

15. Dave Miller, Piloting the Strait, Sain Pub. Co., Pulaski, TN, 1996, p. 440
16. Wayne Jackson, The Existence of God, Haun Pub. Co., Pasadena, TX, 1980, p. 9
17. Werner Keller, The Bible as History, William Morrow and Co., New York, New York, 1956, p. 376
18. William Whiston (translator), Complete Works of Flavius Josephus, Kregel Publications, Grand Rapids, Michigan, 1964, p. 640

CHAPTER 10
WHY DOESN'T THE CHURCH OF CHRIST USE INSTRUMENTAL MUSIC IN WORSHIP?

When one visits the services of the Church of Christ, perhaps the first thing they notice is that the singing is a cappella, that is, without the accompaniment of musical instruments. Since most religious groups worship with the instrument, many are surprised that we do not. The question then comes, *"Why doesn't the Church of Christ use instrumental music?"* It is undoubtedly true that most honest and sincere people have never really stopped to consider this a practice to be questioned. As we approach the study of church music, it is important to determine in advance that the conclusions we reach will not to be based on what we enjoy or what is pleasing to us, but rather what is pleasing and acceptable to God.

Sometimes we hear people say that the Church of Christ does not have music in their worship. This is not true. Virtually every worship service of the church includes music in the authorized form of congregational singing, (Eph. 5:9, Col. 3:16). It is further incorrect to say that members of the church must not like instrumental music because instruments are not used in our worship. Many members have pianos or organs in their own homes and find their use very enjoyable. But, when the members come to worship the Lord, those instruments are left behind. In worshipping the Lord acceptably we must strive not to please ourselves, but the Lord. The only way that we can learn what pleases the Lord is from a study of His Word.

We would like to respond to the question, **"Why doesn't the Church of Christ use instrumental music?"** by discussing six arguments that are often presented by those who attempt to justify the use of the instrument in worship.

Argument Number One: "The New Testament Does Not Forbid the Use of Instrumental Music in Worship."

This is perhaps the most argument that is made in an attempt to justify the use of the instrument in worship. While it is true that the New Testament does not say *"You shall not use instruments of music in your worship,"* this does not give us the liberty to add them. If this reasoning were followed with other items of worship, we could add anything that pleases us, as long as it wasn't specifically prohibited, and still be pleasing to God.

The Law of Exclusion Must Be Observed

An example of the law of exclusion is seen in the instructions regarding the Lord's Supper. The New Testament does not say, *"You shall not have beef steak and coffee as elements in the Lord's Supper."* A positive command or approved example does not have to be followed with a list of things that are not allowed. The elements of the Lord's supper are clearly specified as *"bread"* and *"fruit of the vine"* (Matt. 26:26-30). It was not necessary for the Lord to then list all the things that we could not use as elements in the Lord's Supper. That list would be endless. By telling us what is to be included, this automatically excludes all else.

The Specified Music

Vocal music is one type of music and instrumental music is another. When it comes to music in New Testament worship we have been told the kind of music that we are to offer. That music was specified as vocal. *"Teaching and admonishing one another in psalms and hymns and spiritual songs, singing with grace in your hearts to the Lord,"* (Col. 3:16 NKJV). And again, *"Speaking to one another in psalms and hymns and spiritual songs, singing and making melody in your heart to the Lord,"* (Eph. 5:19). No one ever denies that we are worshipping in truth when we sing to the Lord. No one ever suggests that vocal music be eliminated in favor of instrumental music in order to be more pleasing to the Lord.

Instrumental Music

In addition to Col. 3:16 and Eph. 5:19, passages pertaining to music in worship can be found in Matt. 26:30, Mark 14:26, Acts 16:25, Rom. 15:9, I Cor. 14:15, and Heb. 2:12. In each and every case the type of music was vocal. In none of these references is there a mention of the use of musical instruments. We have authority for vocal music, but we have no authority to offer any other kind of music.

Nadab and Abihu

In the Old Testament this principal of exclusion is seen in several incidents. One of these is the example of Nadab and Abihu. They *"offered profane fire before the Lord, which He had not commanded them"* (Lev. 10:1-2). It was not necessary for them to have a commandment that said *"You shall not offer profane fire,"* for when these men were told what fire to offer, it excluded all others. Unfortunately, they offered what they wanted and not what the Lord wanted, and they lost their lives because of their disobedience.

The Lord never authorized instrumental music in worship. No apostle ever sanctioned it. No New Testament writer ever commanded it or condoned it.

Argument Number Two: "But, Hasn't the Church Always Used Instrumental Music in Worship?"

Most definitely, the church has not always used instrumental music in worship. One may read everything that the New Testament has to say about church music but he will not read anything about the use of a musical instrument.

Only Vocal Music

The early church, as it existed in the time of the apostles, did not use instruments in worship. In fact, historians agree that the instrument was not brought into the worship of God until hundreds of years after Jesus and the apostles died. The fact that the church of the first century did not use instrumental music in their worship is powerful evidence that we have no business today assuming that it is proper and inserting it into our worship.

A Cappella

The Latin *"a cappella"* was carried over into our language to describe vocal singing without the accompaniment of instruments. While this phrase is commonly used for this purpose, it is interesting to know its origin. "*A cappella* literally says in Latin, 'as in the church (or chapel).' This too shows that for many centuries the church sang its praises to God without accompaniment, and that practice was so consistent and uniform that the phrase 'as in the church' came to mean 'unaccompanied singing.'" (Praising God With Thankful Hearts, G. and H. Hougey, p. 7).

Were Instruments in Existence?

Some may be wondering if musical instruments were even in existence at the time of the establishment of the church. Yes, most definitely, musical instruments had been in existence for thousands of years before the church was established. They were even used in the Old Testament under the Law of Moses by some of the same people who became Christians and refused to have them as a part of their Christian worship. Those who lived as contemporaries of the apostles and other early church leaders understood that the instrument had no place in the worship of the church.

When Were Instruments Introduced into Worship?

As to the time when the instrument was adopted into so called Christian worship, the American Encyclopedia, Volume 12, page 688 states, "*Pope Vitalian is related to have first introduced organs into some of the churches of Western Europe about A.D. 670.*" Even in the Roman Catholic Church the introduction of the instrument caused such a furor that it was removed and not reinstated until about 130 years later. In the Eastern or Greek Orthodox Church the instrument is still not used in their worship services in Europe. In the United States the Greek Orthodox Church rejected its use in worship until about the middle of the twentieth century.

Argument Number Three: "Instrumental Music Was Used in the Old Testament."

It is true that instrumental music was used in the Old Testament. However, simply because the musical instruments were used in Old Testament times in some cases does not justify their use in worshipping under the Christian dispensation. It is interesting to note that even in the Old Testament under the Law of Moses the instruments of music were not used without restriction.

The Use of Instruments Was Restricted Even Under Old Covenant

"*The Jews did not use mechanical instruments of music in the tabernacle and the synagogue worship, although it was used in the temple. Church Music in History and Practice, page 15, by Winford C. Douglas, states: 'The synagogue music was an adoption, without musical instruments, of the Temple music.' In McClintock and Strong Encyclopedia Vol. 6, page 762, it is stated: 'The instruments were never used in ancient worship.'*" (Mechanical Instruments of Music in Worship, page 9 by V.E. Howard.)

Can Everything in Old Testament Worship Be Brought Over into the New Testament Church?

The answer to that question is **No!** Many things that were practiced during the dispensation of the Old Covenant are not included under the church of the New Testament. Circumcision, animal sacrifices, offering of the blood of bulls and goats, burning of incense, and observance of the Sabbath are but a few of the things that were approved in the Old Testament that cannot be practiced in the New Testament church. If we return to the Old Testament in order to justify the use of musical instruments in our worship today, we can also go there to justify circumcision, animal sacrifices, offering the blood of bulls and goats, burning of incense, and observance of the Sabbath in our worship today. But, we do not have authority to practice any of those things today because we are under a different law, the New Covenant given by Jesus Christ (Heb. 8:6-13).

We Are Not Under the Old Law

The Law of Moses was given to the Jews until Christ should come (Gal. 3:19-26). After Christ came, the Old Law was taken out of the way (Col. 2:14). Therefore, today we must go to the New Testament to learn how to acceptably worship God. When we do so, we find absolutely no authority for using the instrument in worship.

Argument Number Four: "Instrumental Music Is Simply an Aid to Singing."

Many sincere worshippers are convinced that musical instruments are not a part of the worship, but are simply aids. They place instruments of music in the same category as songbooks and pitch pipes. However, the songbook produces no sound, and the pitch pipe is silent before the singing begins. However, unlike these true aids, the instrument produces music that becomes a part of the worship.

Musical Instruments Are Not Simply Aids

If instruments are only aids in worship today, as some contend, what is done with instruments today that was not done with them in

Jewish worship? In the Jewish worship the sound of the instruments became a part of the worship. Nothing is done to the instruments today to change that. They enter into the worship today just as they did in the Jewish worship.

Musical Instruments Were a Part of Worship

Please consider the following Old Testament passages to clearly see that the sound of the instrument was indeed a part of the worship and not simply an aid. *"And the Levites stood with the musical instruments of David, and the priests with the trumpets. Then Hezekiah gave the order to offer the burnt offering on the altar. When the burnt offering began, the song to the Lord also began with the trumpets, accompanied by the instruments of David, king of Israel. While the whole assembly worshipped, the singers also sang and the trumpets sounded; all this continued until the burnt offering was finished"* (2 Chron. 29:26-28, NASB). In this passage it is demonstrated that the music of the instrument became a part of the worship. The instruments of music played a prominent role in this worship scene as did the burnt offering and the singing.

"Praise Him with the Harp"

The Psalmist declared *"Praise Him with trumpet sound. Praise Him with harp and lyre. Praise Him with timbrel and dancing. Praise Him with stringed instruments and pipe. Praise Him with loud cymbals. Praise Him with resounding cymbals"* (Psalms 150:3-5). Can anyone deny that the instruments were used in offering praise? One cannot have it both ways. If an instrument is used in offering praise, then it cannot be merely an aid. God's

Word simply declares that when instrumental music was used in the worship, it was a part of that worship and no amount of wishful thinking can conceal that fact. We hasten to add that the praise that was offered in the passages cited was done under the Mosaic dispensation. We live in the Christian age in which there is no authority for worshipping with the instrument.

What Is an Aid?

An aid is something that will help you do the thing that the Lord has directed without adding an element to the thing commanded. When God told Noah to *"Make for yourselves an ark of gopher wood"* (Gen. 6:14), He specified the type of wood, but that did not eliminate aids. As an aid he could use a hammer in the construction of the ark, but with the use of this aid the ark would still be made of gopher wood. However if Noah had added oak, walnut or any other kind of wood, the ark would not have been made according to God's will. These unauthorized elements could not be properly classified as aids.

Lord's Supper

In the Lord's Supper we use the fruit of the vine and the bread. Those are the only ingredients that have been specified (I Cor. 11:26). A plate to hold the bread and a container to hold the fruit of the vine would be considered as aids. However, if another type of food were added to the Lord's Supper it would be an addition and not an aid. That is exactly what is done when an instrument of music is added to the singing in worship. An unauthorized element is added.

Argument Number Five: "Since The Bible Speaks of Harps in Heaven, We Should Be Able to Have Instruments in Our Church Worship."

In an effort to justify instrumental music in worship, some turn to the Book of Revelation and cite scriptures there that speak of harps in heaven. They then conclude that if harps are in heaven then pianos and organs can be used in our worship here on earth.

Figurative Language

The Book of Revelation is highly symbolic and speaks of many things in figurative language. John saw spiritual things in heaven and described them in symbols by comparing them to material things that are understandable to us, things of great beauty, grandeur, and awe. In this way John related to us things that could not be framed in our limited language.

There are many things in heaven that are mentioned in Revelation that are unquestionably figurative, such as horses, sickles, incense, fire, bowls, a sea of glass mixed with fire, a woman clothed with the sun and the moon under her feet, a red dragon, jasper walls, a golden street, and beasts. It is just as logical to make every one of these things literal as is it is make the harps literal.

Symbolic for Prayers

The symbolism is clearly shown in the following text usually cited to justify instrumental music by showing that it speaks of harps, *"... the four living creatures and the twenty-four elders fell down before the Lamb, each having harp, and golden bowls full of incense, which are the prayers of the saints."* (Rev. 5:8) The *"golden bowls full of incense"* is identified as being symbolic of the prayers of the saints. If the *"bowls"* are symbolic isn't it logical to conclude that the harps are also figurative?

"Like the Sound of Harpists"

Another favorite passage of those who advocate instrumental music in worship is the recording of the vision of John in Rev. 14:2: *"And I heard a voice from heaven, like the sound of many waters and like the sound of loud thunder, and the voice which I heard was like the sound of harpists playing their harps"* (NASB). John does not say that there were *"many waters"* or *"loud thunder"* or *"harps,"* but a sound like these things. It is interesting that some, who want to make the harps literal, make no such attempt regarding the waters and the thunder. Obviously, all three are figurative.

Literal Harps in Spiritual Realm?

Heaven is a spiritual realm made of spiritual beings (Heb. 12:23). What would literal harps be doing in a spiritual realm? Are we to suppose that heaven will have forests for wood, lumber mills, steel companies, and factories to manufacture and assemble instruments? Will there be repair shops when strings are broken or parts are needed? No serious Bible student would for a moment consider such to be the case. Those who want the Scriptures to teach that there are literal harps in heaven perhaps have not considered how unreasonable such a position really is.

Figurative Harps Do Not Justify Literal Pianos

Furthermore, even if there were literal harps in heaven, a spiritual kingdom, this would still not justify the use of instruments of music in worship here on earth. The principle of acceptable worship is not altered by what will or will not be in heaven. Heaven and the church on earth are two different realms. In heaven there will be no marriage or giving in marriage, but this does not abolish marriage here. In heaven the street is described as pure gold, but we do not attempt to reproduce that street here. In heaven there will be no baptism, but it is commanded here. In heaven we will not observe the Lord's Supper, but the Lord has commanded it here.

It is far-fetched to conclude that the references to figurative harps in heaven gives us the right to add instrumental music to our singing praises to God in worship in the church. *"And in vain they worship Me, teaching as doctrines the commandments of men"* (Matt. 15:9).

Argument Number Six: "The Greek Word 'Psallo' Justifies Instrumental Music In Worship."

In more recent years one will sometimes hear the argument that the Greek word *"psallo"* is justification for using mechanical instruments of music in worship. A form of the word *"psallo"* occurs in Ephesians 5:19 where it is translated as *"making melody."* Since the meaning of the word is to *"pluck, pull, twang,"* some who are hopeful that an instrument is meant here, jump to the conclusion that mechanical instruments of music are here authorized. However, if one reads the remaining part of that sentence, the instrument with which the *"melody"* is to be made is the human heart. *"Singing and making melody in your heart to the Lord."*

Instrument Mandatory?

If the word *"psallo"* in Ephesians means to play a stringed instrument, then it would be imperative for each individual in the worship assembly to play an instrument in the worship. You could no more leave out the instrument than you could leave out the singing. The word is imperative and cannot merely permit the instrument; it would make it mandatory.

Ephesians 5:19 Is Vocal Music

The apostles and inspired writers of the New Testament understood Greek and wrote in Greek. They certainly understood *"psallo."* It is significant that in the years following the establishment of the church, they never gave the slightest indication that there was any teaching from the Lord that would include instrumental music in worship. Paul wrote Ephesians 5:19 by the inspiration of the Holy Spirit and he could not have intended *"psallo"* to include singing with the accompaniment of instruments. If so, he would have made sure that all the congregations used stringed instruments in their worship. But, such did not happen. From internal and external evidences we can easily conclude that the church of the New Testament certainly did not use instrumental music with their worship.

They Understood "Psallo"

The Greek Orthodox Church certainly should understand the Greek language. Even to the present day they still reject instrumental music in worship in Europe. They should have been able to know if *"psallo"* included the instrument. Obviously they knew that it did not and therefore rejected the instrument. The Greek Orthodox Church in the United States rejected the use of the instrument in worship until near the middle of the 20th century when some of their congregations started to use it. When they adopted it, it was not because they suddenly understood what the Greek word *"psallo"* meant, but rather they admitted it was because of the influence of the *"Western Church."* (This historical information was confirmed by a conversation between the author and an official of the Greek Orthodox Church, San Francisco Diocese, January 23, 1997).

We Are to Walk by Faith

When it comes to worshipping the God of heaven, we must be very careful that we walk by faith. *"So then faith comes by hearing and hearing by the Word of God"* (Rom. 10:17). We cannot walk by faith if we go beyond that which the Lord has authorized. Walking by faith means that we do *"not exceed what is written"* (I Cor. 4:6).

Vain Worship

When we worship according to our own dictates, we are entering into the area of vain worship. *"And in vain they worship Me, teaching as doctrines the commandments of men"* (Matt. 15:9). Instrumental music was left out of the New Testament church because the Lord did not want it there. Men are presumptuous to place their own likes and desires above those that the Lord has authorized. When they do so, they are guided by the wisdom of men and not by the wisdom of God.

Honoring the Silence of the Scriptures

The New Testament is our rule of faith and practice in all matters pertaining to Christian worship. We must speak where the Word speaks and remain silent where it is silent. Since the Word is silent concerning the use of instrumental music in Christian worship services, disciples who are concerned with worshipping the Lord acceptably in faith must worship without the addition of unauthorized instruments.

CHAPTER 11
WHAT IS THE ROLE OF WOMEN IN THE CHURCH?

There is growing pressure in the Lord's church for women to assume leadership roles in the church as well as the public worship. Without question the influence of society and culture is having an effect on God's people. Up until a few years ago we did not have difficulty in understanding what the Scriptures taught on this subject. It was generally viewed that the Scriptures presented certain limitations for women and those limitations were understood and accepted. Unfortunately, in recent years some have rejected those limitations and are now attempting to place women in leadership roles. As a result, this matter has developed into an extremely divisive issue that threatens the harmony and purity of the church.

This issue cannot be settled by what is politically correct, or on the basis of what we like or dislike, but rather it must be settled by what the Scriptures have to say. Most definitely, the Bible reveals God's will for women pertaining to their role in the church.

Submission

Some have suggested that unless a woman can have exactly the same role in the church as the man, she is a second-rate Christian. This is simply not true. Biblical submission does not make anyone a second-rate Christian. Please look at I Corinthians 11:3, *"But I want you to know that the head of every man is Christ, the head of woman is man, and the head of Christ is God"* (NKJV).

This passage tells us that Christ is in submission to God, man is in submission to Christ, and woman is in submission to man. Christ is not a second-rate savior because he is in submission to God. The man is not a second-rate Christian because he is in submission to Christ, and the woman is not a second-rate Christian because she is in submission to man. Certainly, she has a different role than does the man, but this does not make her inferior.

What Women CAN Do

Before we notice limitations that apply to women, we should first observe some of the things that women can and should do. Because they have some limitations does not mean that women are to be inactive in the church. On the contrary, Christian women play a vital role in the life of every congregation.

A Christian woman is to teach other women, love her children, be discreet, be chaste, be a homemaker, be good, and be obedient to her own husband (Titus 2:4-5). She can teach children (2 Tim. 3:15). She can teach men privately (Acts 18:26). She can do good works, raise children, lodge strangers, wash the feet of the saints, relieve the afflicted (I Tim. 5:10). She can marry, bear children, manage the house, and give no opportunity to the adversary (I Tim. 5:15). She can be submissive to her husband, winning over the non-Christian husband to the Lord by her godly conduct (I Pet. 3:1).

To their great credit, Christian women engage quietly in many good works of benevolence that brings glory to the Lord. They care for the needy and visit the sick. They provide transportation for the elderly, taking them to purchase their groceries and to keep medical appointments. They comfort the bereaved, prepare food, clean houses for the disabled, and do a host of other chores. Much of the work done in the local congregation would simply not be done if it were not for the women. Women are worthy of great honor for all that they do!

What Women CANNOT Do
(I Timothy 2:7-15)

In the second and third chapters of First Timothy, Paul deals with how one should conduct himself in *"the house of God, which is the church of the living God, the pillar and ground of the truth"* (I Tim. 3:15). Prior to Paul's discussion of the role of women he boldly establishes his authority as an apostle and his right to speak. He is not offering his opinion, as some have suggested, but is speaking with the authority of inspiration: *"For which I was appointed a preacher and an apostle – I am speaking the truth in Christ and not lying – a teacher of the Gentiles in faith and truth"* (I Tim. 2:7).

Public Prayer

The *"therefore"* in verse 8 and what follows is directly related to Paul's claim to be speaking the truth as an apostle of Jesus. Paul then clarifies that the men are to do the public praying: *"I desire therefore that the men pray everywhere, lifting up holy hands, without wrath and doubting"* (I Timothy 2:8).

The offering of public prayers in the assemblies is authorized for men only. In view of the fact that women were to worship (John 4:23-24, Acts 2:42), and that women prayed in certain situations (I Corinthians 11:5,13), verse 8 must refer to the men having the responsibility of leading in the offering of prayers when both men and women were present.

Women to Adorn Themselves

"In like manner also, that the women adorn themselves in modest apparel ... which is proper for women professing godliness, with good works" (I Tim. 2:9-10).

Paul begins his discussion of the women by saying *"In like manner also."* That same apostolic authority that was used to direct what men are to do, is the same now used to give direction for the women. While men are to lead in prayer, women are to adorn themselves modestly and live lives in which they manifest good works.

Women Not Permitted to Teach Men

Paul then reminds Timothy of the need for Christian women to learn in silence with a submissive attitude:

"Let a woman learn in silence with all submission. And I do not permit a woman to teach or to have authority over a man, but to be in silence" (I Tim. 2:11-12).

In spite of the fact that Paul is making this pronouncement with authority as an apostle of Jesus, it is amazing that some people today simply dismiss it as one would do with an unwelcome opinion offered by an unqualified person!

Learn in Silence

These instructions apply to all women for all time. Women were not only to dress in modest apparel, behave with godliness and good works, they were to *"learn in silence with all submission"* (I Tim. 2:12). Since women are to sing (Eph. 5:19) and confess Christ (Rom. 10:9-10), the restriction on women remaining silent obviously does not extend to these activities. However, when an assembly of men and women is gathered together for teaching by a selected teacher, that teacher must be a man. It is impossible to deliver a public lesson without the audience submitting to the speaker. A woman must not assume the designated authority necessary to teaching, but she is to assume the submissive role along with the others assembled.

Can Women Be Given the Authority?

The restriction given in verse 12 regarding the male/female relationships has two parts: (1) *"I do not permit a woman to teach,"* (2) *"or to have authority over a man."* As observed earlier, there are times when women are authorized to teach. The restriction then must have to do with teaching over a man. She is not to have authority over a man in any sense that would violate these scriptures.

Some have argued that a woman cannot take authority over a man, but if she is given that authority by the men, she would not violate this passage. However appealing that may sound, since God did not give women that authority, they cannot have it, no matter what a group of men might decide. It is improper for women to place themselves, or allow themselves to be placed in a public position of teaching men or teaching a mixed group of men and women. The total context of all passages dealing with the role of women in the church clearly shows that they did not take a leading role in praying or teaching over men.

Not a Matter of Culture

In order to justify women taking leadership roles today, some argue that the restrictions given by Paul were just cultural in nature and applied only to the women of that time and place. However wishful some may be, this kind of thinking cannot be substantiated by the Scriptures. There are three primary New Testament passages in which the apostle discusses feminine restrictions and subjection. They are I Corinthians 11:2-16; I Corinthians 14:33-38; and I Timothy 2:11-15. A summary of these passages reveal that Paul's inspired reasons for requiring such subjection had absolutely nothing to do with culture or custom. The fact that present social attitudes are opposed to what is taught in the New Testament about women does not in the least change what the Bible says.

This letter to the Corinthians was not written to the Corinthians exclusively. It was addressed to *"all who in every place call on the name of Jesus Christ our Lord"* (1:2). This shows clearly that the instructions were for all Christians in all places for all times.

Further, there can be no doubt that Paul's instructions for women given through Timothy in I Tim. 12:11-15 are intended to be for all women. Paul gives two reasons for the restrictions being placed on women and neither of them has anything to do with custom or culture. The first reason given for this restriction is the order of creation:

"For Adam was formed first, then Eve" (I Tim. 2:13).

Adam had priority in creation. He was the original human being. Eve was taken from Adam, being formed as a helper to him. She was subordinate to him. This argument based on priority of creation is strengthened by Paul's statement to the Christians in Corinth:

> *"For man is not from woman, but woman from man. Nor was man created for the woman, but woman for the man"* (I Cor. 11:8-9)

The teaching of Paul regarding the public position of the woman in which she holds a subordinate position to man is not based upon custom, culture, or human decision, but upon God's divine order of creation.

The second reason that Paul gives for excluding the woman from public praying and teaching is the fact that Eve was deceived by Satan back in the garden of Eden (Gen. 3:1-6).

> *"And Adam was not deceived, but the woman being deceived, fell into transgression"* (I Tim. 2:14).

Both sinned, but Eve was thoroughly deceived by Satan, while Adam followed Eve in the sin with his eyes open. In this important situation in which Eve was placed she showed that she was not qualified to take the lead. Paul recognized that there was a distinction between the masculine and feminine natures. So, according to inspired teaching, the woman is not to be the leader, but is to be in subjection to the man.

RULES FOR WOMEN IN THE ASSEMBLY
(I Corinthians 14:34-35)

When the Apostle Paul wrote to the church in Corinth he gave clear and specific instruction concerning the role of women in the public assembly:

> *"Let your women keep silent in the churches, for they are not permitted to speak; but they are to be submissive, as the law also says"*
> *(I Cor. 14:34).*

Such phrases as *"if the whole church comes together"* (v. 23), *"Whenever you come together"* (v. 26), *"in the churches"* (v. 34), and *"In church"* (v. 35) clearly show that the speaking limitation placed on women was intended to be in the church assembly. This rule of women remaining silent is positive, explicit and universal. There is no ambiguity here. Those who would advocate change in the role of women in the church today may make some plausible sounding arguments from a human standpoint, but the authority of the inspired apostle remains positive: *"Let your women keep silent in the churches, for they are not permitted to speak"* (v. 34).

Abuses in the Worship Services

During the infancy of the church some Christians were given special miraculous gifts that enabled them to do things they could not otherwise do. The Corinthian church had several of these gifts, but there were restrictions governing their usage. In I Corinthians chapters 12-14 Paul wrote to correct certain abuses that had crept into the worship of the church at Corinth. Part of those abuses in worship involved the misuse of miraculous gifts. Besides speaking in languages that no one in the assembly knew, and more than one person speaking at the same time, some women were speaking out publicly in the worship. Paul wrote to identify and correct these abuses.

While gifted men were allowed to speak in the public assembly in foreign languages (tongues) as long as an interpreter was present, and other men were allowed to prophesy in the public assembly in an orderly fashion, women were restricted. The women were to keep silent and take no part in this. That which constituted the business of the public teaching was reserved for male members only. The special gifts that were present in the church at Corinth are no longer with us today, but the principle remains. The public teaching in the assembly is reserved for the male members of the church.

Ask Their Husbands at Home

"And if they want to learn something, let them ask their own husbands at home" (I Cor. 14:35).

The Christian women at Corinth were not to interrupt the public worship. Rather, if they wanted to learn more on a particular subject or have their questions answered, they were to inquire of their husbands when they got home. But, what if a woman was not married? Since the reference to women is general, it is possible to conclude that the word here means men in general. Nevertheless, it is likely that most of the women were married and did have husbands at home to answer their questions. If they were not married, they surely had some man in their family or circle of friends to whom they could direct their questions and not disrupt the services. This could be an uncle, brother, friend, elder, or preacher.

Shameful for Women to Speak

Paul then states one more reason for the women to remain silent in the worship assembly: *"for it is shameful for a women to speak in church"* (I Cor. 14:35). It would not be shameful for a woman to sing when all others are singing, or make the confession of her faith prior to baptism, but it would be disgraceful for her to speak in teaching over a man. A proper understanding of I Corinthians 14:34-35 and I Timothy 2:11-12 will forever keep Christian women from occupying the pulpit if they intend to be faithful to the Lord.

Division Is Evil

Those who insist on *"modernizing"* the role of women in the church are causing needless division in the Lord's body. One gets the impression that to some causing division is of less concern than allowing women to take leadership roles. To encourage or condone such a practice knowing that it will divide the church cannot be justified. The sin of division is looked upon by the Lord as a very serious matter. In Romans 16:17 Paul said:

> *"Now I urge you, brethren, note those who cause divisions and offenses, contrary to the doctrine which you learned, and avoid them."*

Again, it was the apostle Paul who spoke against division when he wrote to the Corinthians:

> *"Now I plead with you, brethren, by the name of our Lord Jesus Christ, that you all speak the same thing, and that there be no divisions among you, but that you be perfectly joined together in the same mind and in the same judgment" (I Cor. 1:10).*

More Attempts to Justify Women Preachers

In addition to those arguments already discussed that some have offered for placing women in the public worship as leaders and preachers, we notice a few more:

Argument: Since I Corinthians 11:5 speaks of women in the church at Corinth praying and prophesying, why shouldn't women be allowed to do the same thing today?

Response: This passage must be viewed in harmony with clear and explicit restrictions that women were to remain silent in the church. During the infancy of the church some women were given special spiritual gifts. Those gifts are no longer possessed by women or men today (I Cor. 13:8-10), so whatever the situation was at Corinth it cannot be duplicated today. In fact, I Corinthians 11:5 does not fall in the midst of Paul's instructions regarding assembly abuses. These do not begin until 11:17. Therefore, this passage seems better fitted to apply to something other than the public assembly.

Since women were prohibited from being teachers of men, it is reasonable to conclude that the women in question used their gifts acceptably in private situations or in assemblies of other women. When men were present in the mixed assemblies, the women were obligated to *"keep silence in the church"* (I Cor. 14:34) since *"it is shameful for a woman to speak in church"* (I Cor. 14:35). While it is clear that women of the first century church did prophesy, it is equally clear and certain that they did not subordinate men to the role of students.

Argument: Galatians 3:28 says that in Christ *"There is neither male nor female."* Therefore, some argue, anything a man can do, can also be done by a woman.

Response: The fact that a woman enjoys the same salvation in Christ, and the same relationship to God as her father, does not change her natural relationship to man that was established by God. In addition, it does not remove restrictions that were placed on women by the inspired apostle Paul.

Argument: In Acts 18:26 it states that Pricilla, a woman, participated with her husband, Aquila, in teaching Apollos.

Response: There can be no justification from this passage for women teaching or preaching in the public assembly of the church. Aquila and Pricilla *"took him aside and explained the way of the Lord more accurately."* This teaching was done in private. It has no reference to public preaching or teaching of men by women. Most certainly a wife can join with her husband today and privately teach a man.

Argument: Romans 16:1 says: *"I commend to you Phoebe our sister, who is a servant of the church in Cenchrea."* Some versions have the word *"deaconess"* as a footnote or marginal note in reference to the word *"servant."* From this, some want to conclude that Phoebe held an office in the church. Therefore, they argue, women should be allowed to do so today.

Response: The word that is translated *"servant"* by almost all translations identified Phoebe not as an official, but one who served the church as a servant. In fact, the Greek word *"diakonos,"* from which we get *"deacon,"* simply means *"servant."* If it is to be understood as meaning anything in an official sense it must be borne out in the context, as was done in Philippians 1:1 and I Timothy 3:8,12. In these passages it obviously is used in the official sense, and is therefore translated *"deacon."* Phoebe had simply been a helper of Paul and others. There is not the slightest evidence that she was a church leader in the official sense. Untold numbers of Christian women today are working and helping in the Lord's work just as Phoebe did then. Surely, no one would suggest that they must hold an office in order function as faithful servants. The office of deacon is reserved for men only. When Paul gave the qualifications for deacons he forever excluded women by saying: **"Let deacons be the husband of one wife"** (I Tim. 3:12).

Argument: Romans 16:7 speaks of a woman named Junia as being an apostle. Therefore, some argue that women can be church leaders and preachers today.

Response: We offer three possible explanations of Romans 16:7. (1) There is no way to prove that Junia was a woman. In the Greek the name is *"Junian."* The gender is not evident. There is just as much reason to believe this person was a man as there is to believe this was a woman, and there is certainly no way to prove that this was a woman. (2) The text does not say that Junia or Junias was an apostle, but rather was *"of note among the apostles."* The meaning is that this person was well known among the apostles, was appreciated by the apostles, rather than being an apostle. (3) The word *"apostle"* comes from the Greek *"apostolos"* which means *"messenger"* or *"one sent."* There are times when the word is used simply to refer to a messenger and does not designate one in the official sense. John 13:16 and 2 Corinthians 8:23 are examples. In Romans 16:17 *"apostle"* may simply refer to a messenger.

Argument: Phil. 4:2-3 says that Euodia and Syntyche labored with Paul in the gospel.

Response: It is far-fetched to suggest that because they helped Paul that they were preachers or even in positions of authority.

Countless thousands have been of assistance to gospel preachers without themselves being public speakers.

Argument: Some women in the Old Testament prophesied. Therefore, some argue, women can be public speakers today.

Response: While we will briefly examine these cases in the Old Testament, the reader must be reminded that we no longer live under the Old Law. If we were, we would still be burning incense in worship and offering animal sacrifices. The Old Law in its entirety was taken out of the way and nailed to the cross (Colossians 2:14). Old Testament cases of women prophets:

1. Miriam prophesied, but she did so with the women. Exodus 15:20 says, *"All the women went out after her..."* There is no indication that Miriam preached or prophesied before men.

2. Huldah was a prophetess, but the only record we have of her prophesying was when men went to her privately (2 Kings 22:14-20). There is no evidence of public preaching here.

3. Anna was a prophetess who stayed in the temple (Luke 2:36-38). She likely stayed in the women's quarters, separated from the men. There is absolutely no suggestion here that Anna publicly prophesied to mixed audiences of men and women.

4. Deborah was a prophetess in the hill country of Ephraim, but there is no indication that she publicly proclaimed God's word to the multitudes. On the contrary, Judges 4:5 says: *"And the children of Israel came up to her for judgment."* To go to such passages as this to justify women preachers today is an extremely weak argument. Even if it could be proved that women were allowed to preach in the

Old Testament, this would have no bearing on what women are allowed to do under the New Testament.

Conclusion

The passages pertaining to the women's role in the church exclude women from preaching, serving as elders or deacons, and leading singing in mixed assemblies of men and women. These passages also exclude women from teaching classes where men are present. In spite of what many are advocating today, within and without the church, the Scriptures do not change. If we want to be the true church of the New Testament, we must heed the instructions of the New Testament, regardless of what pressures are applied for us to be *"politically correct."* The church has always struggled to be in the world, but not be of the world. The mission of the church is to preach the gospel and transform the world, not to be conformed to the world. Paul warned Christians of all times: "And do not be conformed to this world, but be transformed by the renewing of your mind" (Rom. 12:2).

CHAPTER 12
THE "GIFT" OF TONGUES: ECSTATIC UTTERANCE OR ACTUAL LANGUAGE?

The Purpose of Spiritual Gifts

Before the will of the Lord was completely revealed in the form of the New Testament, many Christians of the first century were given special spiritual gifts. These gifts were to aid them during the infancy period of the church when they only knew God's will in part, *"For we know in part and we prophesy in part."* (I Corinthians 13:9). These gifts were of great benefit during the first years of the church, but they were never intended to last forever, *"But where there are prophecies, they will fail; whether there are tongues, they will cease."* (I Corinthians 13:8).

The Gift Most Desired

Of the nine spiritual gifts listed by Paul in I Corinthians 12:8-10, none today is sought after more intensely by some than is the gift of *"tongues."* While those who seek to speak in *"tongues"* may well be honest and sincere, they are misguided for at least two reasons. First, they are misguided because they believe that the gift of *"tongues"* in New Testament times was ecstatic utterance, and secondly, because they believe that the same gift is available today. If we are to understand the Biblical teaching of the gift of *"tongues,"* we must not fall into the trap of trying to make the

Scriptures fit what is practiced in some religious circles today under the name of *"tongues."*

Trained to Speak in "Tongues"?

Typically, the person desiring the gift of *"tongues"* prays that he will receive it. Often this is done under pressure to be like others who have obtained what they consider to be a high spiritual plateau. As foolish and unbiblical as it sounds, this person may even receive training from others regarding his learning now to speak in *"tongues."* He prays hard and desires the gift earnestly. Finally, one day, perhaps after a very intense prayer session, he goes into a hypnotic or trance-like state. From his mouth comes incoherent, nonsensical, *"babbling."* He feels wonderful because he thinks he has "arrived" at last. He thinks he has joined the spiritual elite.

Is Modern "Tongue Speaking" from God?

This phenomenon described above is not from God. It has nothing to do with God. It has nothing to do with the Holy Spirit. The same thing that has been described here and labeled by many as *"tongue speaking"* is also achieved by heathen. Those who absolutely do not believe in the one true God, Jesus Christ, or the Holy Spirit have been able to achieve the same thing. *"Tongues of a sort have been manifested in pagan cults which existed before Christ came to earth, and in others which have not been influenced by Christianity."* [1]

Don't Make the Scriptures Fit the Practice

Many, in approaching the Bible to study this subject, do so presuming that the practice of ecstatic utterance is to be found there.

The "Gift" of Tongues: Ecstatic Utterance or Actual Language?

Most people today have been exposed, in one form or another, to something that they were told was the gift of *"tongues."* Therefore, they are inclined to make the Scriptures fit their preconceived ideas on the subject. When they read a passage where the word *"tongues"* is used, they jump to the conclusion that the inspired writer is talking about the same thing that can be witnessed today in some charismatic churches.

However, if one can leave preconceived ideas behind and approach the Scriptures with a totally open and receptive heart, he can come to a proper understanding of this New Testament gift. He will also come to have an appreciation for the wisdom of the Lord in supplying it during the infancy of the church.

Only a Few Passages Deal with "Tongues"

Many people are surprised to find how little the New Testament has to say about this gift. *"Does it not seem strange indeed that if speaking with tongues was such a vital part of Christian experience, or was to be perpetuated in the church, that so little attention is paid to it by the writers of the New Testament, including Paul, and that he fully appreciated the gift?"* [2]

The Promise of Jesus to the Apostles
Mark 16:14-20

The first time the miraculous gift of *"tongues"* occurs in the New Testament is found in Mark 16:17. This is the only record we have that Jesus made regarding to speaking in *"tongues."* In Mark 16:14 we read that Jesus appeared to his apostles and *"Reproached them for their unbelief and hardness of heart"* (NASB). He then gave them the Great Commission and made them a promise: *"And these signs will accompany those who have believed: in my name* they will cast out demons, they will speak with new tongues; they will pick up serpents, and if they drink any deadly poison, it shall not hurt them; they will lay hands on the sick and they will recover"* (Mark 16:17-18). The fulfillment of this promise to the apostles is found two verses later, *"And they went out and preached everywhere, while the Lord worked with them, and confirmed the word by the signs that followed"* (Mark 16:20).

What About Taking Up Serpents?

Many today who seek to speak in *"tongues"* ignore the facts that this promise was given to the Apostles. They have to ignore this in order to lay claim to *"tongues"* for themselves. However, these same people do not often show the same enthusiasm to taking up serpents, drinking poison, healing the sick, or casting out demons. All of these were a part of the same promise. To be consistent, if one insists that the gift of *"tongues"* is for modern man, then so must the handling of poisonous snakes.

"Under whatever circumstances 'tongues' were given in fulfillment of this passage, at that same time and under those same circumstances there were also to be casting out of demons and healing the sick. It is not fair to the text to claim its tongues without being able to produce the other signs as well." [3]

Events on the Day of Pentecost
Acts 2:1-21
Actual Foreign Languages Were Spoken

In the second passage dealing with *"tongues"* we have the only detailed historical account of the occurrence of *"tongues,"* *"Now there were Jews living in Jerusalem, devout men, from every nation under heaven."* (Acts 2:5). Represented in that great audience on the day of Pentecost were many people from many different nations, speaking different languages. There can be no doubt that the *"tongues"* described in Acts 2 referred to actual foreign languages. Of the apostles, verse 4 states, *"And they were all filled with the Holy Spirit and began to speak with other tongues, as the Spirit was giving them utterance"* (Acts 2:4).

Their Own Languages Were Spoken

There is no possibility that this could be the *"jabber"* that some today call ecstatic utterance, because in verse 6 we read, *"They were each one hearing them speak in his own language"* (Acts 2:6). Also, beginning in verse 8 and continuing through verse 11 we clearly see the various nationalities who were able to hear the gospel preached in their own language, *"And how is it that we each hear them in our own language to which we were born? Parthians and Medes and Elamites, and residents of Mesopotamia, Judea and Cappadocia, Pontus and Asia, Phrygia and Pamphylia, Egypt and the districts of Libya around Cyrene, and visitors from Rome, both Jews and proselytes, Cretans and Arabs – we hear them in our own tongues, speaking of the mighty deeds of God"* (Acts 2:8-11). What a great miracle this was! Each man was privileged to hear the precious, soul saving gospel preached in his own language. This was truly a sign to the unbelievers.

The Clearest Description of "Tongues"

"A comparison with other passages which mention 'glossolalia' (tongue speaking) will show that the clearest description of the nature of tongues is found in Acts 2. In no

other place is there an explicit statement as to the real nature of tongues-speech. Here we see 'glossolalia' in its unperverted form as God intended it... We are therefore justified in viewing the account in Acts 2 as the definitive description of what New Testament "tongues" really were. On this basis we may regard the Acts passage as establishing the guidelines for all later and less obvious references to tongues."* [4] Since Acts 2 gives us the only historical account in any detail, we must learn heavily on this passage for understanding when we later come across less detailed passages relating to *"tongues"* or the *"gift of tongues."*

Not Necessary to Define "Tongues" Each Time

Since the inspired Scriptures have furnished to us a definition of *"tongues"* in this one passage, it is not necessary for all future references regarding the same gift to also be accompanied with detailed account such as provided by Luke in Acts 2. It would only be necessary if the gift of *"tongues"* in a later passage is not the same. If, on the other hand, it is the same gift, then a simple reference to that gift as *"tongues"* is adequate. Such is the case with all remaining references made to *"tongues"* after Acts 2.

The Household of Cornelius
Acts 10:44-47, 11:15-18

In reading Acts 10:1-34, one is impressed with the importance of Peter learning that the Gentiles were indeed to be accepted into the family of God. Under the direction of the Lord, Peter went to the house of the Gentile, Cornelius, and taught him and those with him all that *"had been commanded by the Lord"* (Acts 10:33). Peter had learned his lesson well for he began his teaching by saying, *"I most certainly understand now that God is not one* to show partiality, but in every nation the man who fears Him and does what is right, is welcome to Him" (Acts 10:34-35). But even then God was not through showing Peter and all other Jews that the Gentiles had been accepted.

The Household of Cornelius Spoke in "Tongues"

When the Holy Spirit fell on the Gentiles, they were enabled to speak in *"tongues." "While Peter was still speaking these words, the Holy Spirit fell upon all those who were listening to the message. And all the circumcised believers who had come with Peter were amazed, because the gift of the Holy Spirit had been poured out upon the Gentiles also. For they were hearing them speaking with tongues and exalting God"* (Acts 10:44-46).

Same Gift As That of the Apostles

When Peter returned to Jerusalem, the Jews demanded an accounting for what had happened at the house of Cornelius. He responded by saying, *"And as I began to speak, the Holy Spirit fell upon them, just as He did upon us at the beginning"* (Acts 11:15). Two verses later we read, *"If God therefore gave to them the same gift as He gave to us also after believing in the Lord Jesus Christ, who was I that I could stand in God's way?"* (Acts 11:17).

Reasons to Conclude That "Tongues" of Acts 10 Was the Ability to Speak in Foreign Languages

Although this account does not specifically say that the *"tongues"* here referred to actual languages, that conclusion is inescapable for the following three reasons:

1. The same writer, Luke, who recorded the events of Pentecost in Acts 2, and plainly told us that "tongues" were foreign languages, now simply makes reference to these people speaking in "tongues." He makes no attempt to explain what he means by "tongues" because he has already explained it in detail. Now, if this were a different gift than that of Acts 2, it would only be logical that he would re-define it for us.

2. Luke states in Acts 10:45 that "And all the circumcised believers who had come with Peter were amazed, because the gift of the Holy Spirit had been poured out upon the Gentiles also." The "also" no doubt refers back to the previous out-pouring of the Spirit on the day of Pentecost.

3. In case there is any doubt that the gift given to Cornelius was the same as that on the day of Pentecost, Peter removes that doubt by saying, "If God therefore gave to them the same gift as He gave to us also ..." (Acts 11:17). The gift of Acts 2 gave those who received it the ability to speak in foreign languages that they had never studied. Since the gift given to Cornelius was "the same gift," we can only conclude that he also was given the ability to speak in unstudied languages.

The Giving of Spiritual Gifts to the Gentiles Proved They Were Accepted Equally with the Jews

"This was unmistakable proof that God had accepted the Gentiles equally with the Jews to receive the blessings of the

gospel. Since Peter called this the "same" gift, and in Acts 2, Luke makes it clear that the "tongues" were foreign languages, it seems evident foreign languages are meant here. The same Greek word *"glossa"* is used here for "tongue" as in Acts 2. There is nothing in the context of this passage that could lead anyone to think these were ecstatic utterances" [5].

The Disciples of John the Baptizer
Acts 19:1-7

The fourth occurrence of the miraculous gift of *"tongues"* is also found in the book of Acts. Paul, passing through Ephesus, found twelve disciples who had been baptized by John's baptism. They apparently did not even realize that Jesus had come. After Paul talked to them, they were baptized in the name of Jesus. *"And when Paul had laid his hands upon them, the Holy Spirit came on them, and they began speaking with tongues and prophesying"* (Acts 19:6).

This account does not identify the *"tongues"* spoken of here as being foreign languages. Nor does this passage say that this experience was the same as that of Acts 2 and Acts 10. However, it should be noted that Luke is the one who recorded all three of these incidents. In recording this event at Ephesus, Luke used the same word *"glossa"* as he did in the two previous accounts. Further, Luke made no attempt to distinguish between this incident and those he reported previously. The only logical conclusion that can be drawn is that the gift of *"tongues"* received by the Ephesians in Acts 19 was no different from the gift of *"tongues"* of Acts 2.

Not Ecstatic Utterance

"In light of Luke's clear usage in Acts 2 it seems obvious the same word has the same meaning here and refers to unlearned foreign languages... There is no evidence in the Book of Acts itself that the word "glossa" refers to ecstatic utterance. If one takes the text as it stands seriously, he must let Luke define the meaning of this word in Acts, and he has clearly done this in Acts 2." [6]

"Tongues" of Corinth Are Same As Acts 2
(I Corinthians Chapters 12-14)

In discussing the passages in I Corinthians, the reader is asked to observe that Paul does not attempt to define *"tongues"* in any of the three chapters under consideration. Paul was speaking to the Corinthians regarding something with which they were well acquainted. On the other hand, when Luke wrote the book of Acts, addressing it to Theophilus, he felt it necessary to actually describe the gift.

Without question the early Christians in the book of Acts spoke in foreign languages that they had never studied when they were given the gift of *"tongues."* It is inconsistent and unreasonable to assume that when the Corinthian Christians were given the same gift that they spoke in *"gibberish."*

The greatest difficulty in studying I Corinthians 12-14 is to keep from reading into the passages what is currently being labeled as *"tongues"* by the Pentecostal and Neo-pentecostal groups. If the Bible student is able to disregard current phenomenon from his mind and approach this study with a receptive mind, he should emerge with the correct understanding of the subject.

There Is a Purpose in Relating Each Incident of Tongues

"In Mark there is the promise of 'tongues' from Jesus. In Acts, Luke records 'tongue speaking' at the occasion of the Jews, Gentiles and the followers of John the Baptist coming into the kingdom. In I Corinthians there are problems connected with 'speaking in tongues' that Paul must correct.

In Mark, chapter 16, Mark points out the purpose of 'tongue speaking' as one of the signs to confirm revelation. In Acts, Luke describes the nature of 'tongue' speaking and shows how the gift was received. In I Corinthians, Paul corrects men who are making a mockery of a God-given gift.

One cannot understand the New Testament 'glossa' gift by isolating one passage from the other. All three apostolic men write of the 'glossa' gift from a different perspective. One must take all of the evidence together to understand 'tongue speaking' in the New Testament. There is no evidence that the 'glossa' gift at Corinth was any different from that on Pentecost." [7]

"Unknown Tongues"

A great deal of confusion has been created by the word *"unknown"* which precedes *"tongues"* in the King James Version in I Corinthians 14:2, 4, 13, 19, and 27. If a tongue is *"unknown"* it immediately has an air of mystery and hints of the ecstatic. However, the reader is directed to the fact that *"unknown"* appears in italics and therefore was an addition by the translators. The word *"unknown"* does not appear in the Greek text and should not have been included in this passage. It is most reasonable to conclude that the gift of *"tongues"* refers to actual foreign languages known and used by the various nations.

"Tongues of Angels"

Some have made much to do about the phrase *"Tongues of ... angels"* in I Corinthians 13:1. From the context it is easily seen that Paul is here speaking hypothetically for emphasis in showing the need for love. *"Paul did not actually affirm that some spoke the language of angels. He did say that even if one had such ability, without love he could not please God. A similar concept is found in Galatians 1:8 where Paul wrote of an angel preaching another gospel. Obviously he did not mean angels actually preached to men. He meant even if an angel preached a message other than the gospel, it was not to be accepted."* [8]

"Tongues of Angels" at Corinth

The only instructions we have in the New Testament concerning the use of the gift of *"tongues"* is found in the letter to the Corinthians. The church at Corinth had many problems. They were immature, divided, tolerated immorality, and had confusion in their worship services. *"Problems at Corinth were so numerous and so diverse that Paul's corrective letter to this church has commonly been regarded as a sort of catalog of the sins and remedies of a local church. One wonders if tongues would have been mentioned in even this epistle had the Corinthians not been so confused and abusive regarding their proper use. Even here most of what Paul says about tongues is designed to play down their importance and to urge the Corinthians to completely revamp their attitude toward the gift."* [9]

"Tongues," Not "Jabbering"

Those who hold the view that ecstatic utterance is what is meant by *"tongues"* think they will find support for their position in I Corinthians chapter 14. However, in Corinth the gift still refers to actual languages. *"There is no occasion when the servants of the Lord spoke "jabbering" nonsense which was not any language, but certain ones in the early church were given power to speak in foreign or unknown languages in order that all might hear and understand the truth. What could possibly be the purpose in having God's children make a jabbering noise which no one could understand, and calling it a 'tongue?'"* [10]

Reasons to Conclude "Tongues" in Corinth Were Actual Languages

1. The Promise and the Fulfillment

"The promise that Jesus made in Mark 16:17, "They will speak with new tongues" was first fulfilled on Pentecost in Jerusalem and sometime later at Caesarea at the home of Cornelius. The church in Corinth was not established until Paul's second missionary journey about 51 or 52 AD. It would seem logical that the occurrences must be regarded as being identical.

Since the promise is one, so the fulfillment is one, regardless of the place where or time when the fulfillment occurs. For one to set aside this premise he must show that Jesus made two promises or that the fulfillments are different in kind. The evidence available to us in Scripture will not support either conclusion, as we have shown already. Therefore, we conclude that the fulfillment at Corinth was the same as that which had already taken place on Pentecost." [11]

2. The Theme of I Corinthians Chapter 14 Is Edification of the Church

When we understand that the theme of chapter 14 is edification, the part of Paul's instructions to the Corinthians concerning *"tongue speaking"* becomes quite clear. Notice Paul's emphasis of this theme.

"One who speaks in a tongue edifies himself; but one who prophesies edifies the church. Now I wish that you all spoke in tongues, but even more that you would prophesy; and greater is one who prophesies than one who speaks in tongues, unless he interprets, so that the church may receive edifying. But now, brethren, if I come to you speaking in tongues, what shall I profit you, unless I speak to you either by way of revelation or of knowledge or of prophecy or of teaching?" (I Corinthians 14:4-6).

3. One Cannot Be Edified from Unintelligible Sounds

Paul makes his point by placing himself in the picture. Even if he, an apostle, came speaking with a tongue (foreign language) to the Corinthians, they would receive no edifying unless he interpreted the words of that language as conveying some revelation received from God.

Some who spoke in tongues (foreign languages) could not interpret what they spoke, while others had the gift of interpretation. Paul's primary concern here was that the Christians at Corinth would be edified when they assembled together and someone spoke to them. This is obvious as he continues:

4. All Languages Have Meaning

When Paul stated that there were many kinds of languages in the world and all of them had meaning, he clearly is not talking about a *"gibberish."* He is talking about actual languages. However, if one has the ability to speak in a foreign language that others cannot understand, there is no profit or edification for the hearers.

"There are, perhaps, a great many kinds of languages in the world, and no kind is without meaning. If then, I do not know the meaning of the language I shall be to the one who speaks a Barbarian, and the one who speaks will be a barbarian to me" (I Corinthians 14:10-11).

In verse 19 Paul stated that he would rather speak five words with which he could be understood and which would be profitable for instruction, than to speak ten thousand words *"in a tongue"* or a foreign language that the assembly could not understand.

"Yet even lifeless things, either flute or harp, in producing a sound, if they do not produce a distinction in the tones, for if the bugle produces an indistinct sound, who will prepare himself for battle? So also you, unless you utter by the tongue speech that is clear, how will it be known what is spoken? For you will be speaking into the air." (I Corinthians 14:7-9).

5. The Corinthians Could Control Their "Tongue" Speaking

Those today who say that they speak in *"tongues"* are not able to control their *"babbling."* They like to look at verses 14-15 and conclude that the one speaking in *"tongues"* at Corinth had no control over his speech or even understood what he was saying. Their view seems to be that the person's mind goes into *"neutral"* when he goes into this state. It must be emphasized that whatever people do today, when they go into a trance-like state and *"babble"* out of control, it is not what the Corinthians who had the gift of *"tongues"* were doing.

In looking at Paul's instruction to the Corinthians concerning this gift, it is obvious that they were able to control it. For example, they were to limit the number of speakers to two or three. They were not all to speak at the same time, but they were to take turns. If they could not control themselves, they could not meet these requirements that Paul laid out. Also, they were not to speak at all unless there was interpretation present. This could only be possible if those having the gift could control themselves.

This being the case, what do these two verses mean? *"For if I pray in a tongue, my spirit prays, but my mind is unfruitful. What is the outcome then? I shall pray with the spirit and I shall pray with the mind also; I shall sing with the spirit and I shall sing with the mind also."* (I Corinthians 14:14-15).

"The thought evidently is I will sing as the Spirit directs or inspires, and I will sing in a language that those who hear can understand." 12 *"pray with the spirit means to pray with a spiritual gift or with one's own spirit under the direction of the Holy Spirit; to pray with the understanding means to pray so that others can understand the thoughts of the prayer's mind (14:5). Obviously this demanded interpretation of the prayer offered in a tongue."* [13]

6. The Message Must Be Interpreted or the Speaker Is to Remain Silent

When the Christians at Corinth assembled together and one spoke, prayed, or sang in a *"tongue"* it was not edifying to those present unless the speaker also had the power to interpret, or someone else who was present had that gift. Of course God could understand but the assembly could not, and therefore they could not be edified (I Corinthians 14:2). Those who claim to have the gift of *"tongues"* today are not inclined to be limited by such restrictions, but *"babble"* out of control.

7. The Old Testament Reference Proves That Paul was Talking about Actual Languages, and Not Ecstatic Utterance

As Paul continues his discussion of the gift of *"tongues"* in I Corinthians 14:1, he makes a reference to an Old Testament passage, Isaiah 28:11. It is very significant that Paul draws from Jewish history to teach the Corinthians a lesson by referring to an actual language of a foreign people. *"In the law is written, 'By men of strange tongues and by the lips of strangers I will speak to this people, and even so they will not listen to me' says the Lord"* (I Corinthians 14:21).

The Jews had refused to hear Isaiah in their own language, so God threatened to bring their enemies upon them, specifically the Assyrians, who spoke a language that they could not understand. Does anyone believe that the Assyrians were going to speak in *"gibberish"* or ecstatic utterance? Of course not! The Jews might not be able to understand their language, but nevertheless it was a real language.

8. A Non-intelligible Language Is Not a Blessing

Some take great pride today in that they can *"jabber"* in a series of non-intelligible sounds, as though this is some great spiritual achievement and a blessing to them. But, when Paul made this Old Testament reference, he was not telling them that the Jews would be blessed by not understanding the language.

On the contrary, *"this was a judgment upon them, not a mark of God's pleasure. It was designed as their punishment and not an achievement. From this, Paul is teaching the Corinthians that they might learn it was no mark of divine favor to have teachers whose language they could not understand. They were turning a blessing into a curse. The gift of "tongues" was designed to help in spreading the gospel by enabling Christians to address people of various nations, each in his own language."* [14]

The point that should be clearly understood here is the fact that Paul, in drawing this analogy, made reference to an actual foreign language, no ecstatic utterances or *"jabber."*

9. The Gift of "Tongues" Was a Sign to Unbelievers

In New Testament times when a preacher with the gift of *"tongues"* went out to preach, he could go into strange areas where he did not know the language. He could preach the gospel in the language of the people, a language that he had not studied. This was a very practical gift that was truly a sign to unbelievers.

"So then, tongues are for a sign, not to those who believe, but to unbelievers; but prophesy is for a sign, not to unbelievers, but to those who believe" (I Corinthians 14:22).

There Were Rules for Using "Tongues"

In I Corinthians 14:26-28 Paul sums up the matter of *"tongues"* by giving some rules to the Corinthians about the use of this gift. *"What is the outcome then, brethren? When you assemble, each one has a psalm, has a teaching, has a revelation, has a tongue... has an interpretation. If any one speaks in a tongue, it should be by two or at the most three, and each in turn, and* let one interpret; but if there is no interpreter, let him keep silent in the church."

"There are a number of rules in these two verses which must be observed whenever "tongues" may be used. These are:

1. No more than three may speak in a "tongue" on any given occasion.
2. All "tongue speaking" must be done "in turn," that is by persons speaking one at a time.
3. On no occasion may "tongues" be used unless an interpreter is standing by to tell the audience every word that was spoken." [15]

Tongues Were to Cease

The ability to speak in a language that one had never studied was a marvelous gift that was given to some Christians during the infancy of the church. It was never intended to last forever.

"If there are tongues, they will cease. For we know in part, and we prophesy in part; but when the perfect comes, the partial will be done away" (I Corinthians 13:8-10).

These miraculous gifts were the *"partial"* and they were to disappear when the *"perfect"* was come. The *"perfect"* was the complete will of God revealed to man. When the New Testament was completed there was no longer a need for the "partial" or the miraculous gifts, including the gift of *"tongues."*

Conclusion

The spiritual gifts were performed by the apostles and those on whom the apostles had laid hands and transferred this gift. When the last apostle died and the last person on whom they had laid hands died, the miraculous came to an end. The gift of *"tongues"* was the ability to speak in foreign languages that the recipient had never studied. It was a gift that was never intended to be permanent. It dos not exist today.

Footnotes

1. Bales, James D., Pat Boone and the Gift of Tongues, J.D. Bales, Searcy, Arkansas
2. L'Roy, Elmer, The Holy Spirit, p. 61
3. Fudge, E., Speaking in Tongues, p. 14
4. Burdick, Donald W., Tongues, To Speak or Not to Speak, Moody Press, Chicago, Illinois, p. 16
5. Pack, Frank, Tongues and the Holy Spirit, Biblical Research Press, Abilene, Texas, p. 60.
6. Ibid., p. 63
7. Jividen, Jimmy, Glossolalia, From God or Man? Star Bible Pub., Ft. Worth, Texas, p. 107
8. Allen, Jimmy, Survey of First Corinthians Pub. by Jimmy Allen, Searcy Arkansas, p. 151
9. Fudge, E. P. 20
10. DeHoff, George, Dehoff Pub., Murfreesboro, Tennessee, p. 86
11. Cannon, Bob, Glossolalia Inglewood Church of Christ, Inglewood, CA, p. 12, 13
12. Lipscomb, David, I Corinthians Gospel Advocate Commentaries, Nashville, TN, p. 208
13. Allen, Jimmy, p. 174
14. Cannon, Bob, p. 19
15. Coffman, Burton, Commentary on 1 and 2 Corinthians Firm Foundation Pub. Co, Austin, Texas p. 238

CHAPTER 13
WHY ELDERS IN THE CHURCH?

In order to function properly every organization must have some form of government. The Lord's church is no exception. The church in the universal sense is a divine monarchy, with Jesus as its king. He has all authority in heaven and on earth (Matt. 28:18), and no man or set of men on earth has any right to bind anything upon God's people which Christ has not bound. Yet, the Lord in His wisdom recognized the need for leadership among His people to carry out His purposes here on earth. He has provided that qualified men be set apart to lead and direct the work of each local congregation. Since the New Testament describes this office and gives the qualifications for those who would serve in this capacity, it is essential that we give careful attention to its teaching on the subject.

Scriptural Designations for Elders

The leaders of the local congregation are called by several names, all referring to the same position, but describing different functions. The most common term used is elders. (The Greek is presbuteros from which we get the word presbyter). In Acts 20:17 we read of Paul sending to Ephesus in order to have a meeting with the *"elders of the church."* The word elder suggests one who has maturity, experience, spiritual development, and stability. The word presbyter means the same.

Elders are also called bishops. (The Greek is episkopos from which we get the word episcopal). When Paul wrote to the church in Philippi he addressed his letter to all the saints, *"with the bishops and deacons."* The term overseer means the same as bishop and signifies one who has the oversight of planning and directing the work of the congregation.

In I Peter 5:1-5, the work of the elder is described as that of a shepherd, so elders may correctly be designated as such. J.W. McGarvey said, *"The title 'shepherd' is still more significant than either of the other two. The Jewish shepherd was at once the ruler, the guide, the protector, and the companion of his flock. Often ... he slept upon the ground beside his sheep at night. Sometimes, when prowling wolves came near to rend and scatter the flock, his courage was put to the test. He did not drive them to water and to pasturage; but he called his own sheep by name, so familiar was he with every one of them, and he led them out, and went before them, and the sheep followed him, for they knew his voice."* [1]

The word pastor means the same as shepherd and suggests one who is responsible for feeding and caring for the flock. The word pastor is often misused and applied to the preacher, but it rightfully belongs to each elder who shepherds the flock.

A Choice Not to Have Elders?

In the early years of a congregation, it may be that the church will not have elders for a time because a plurality of the men in the congregation are not qualified to serve in that capacity. Since men are not qualified, the congregation exists scripturally in spite of the fact that they are not fully organized. Such congregations should strive to help brethren within the congregation grow to meet the qualifications set down in the New Testament.

It is unfortunate that some congregations continue without elders long after they have men who have qualified themselves to lead. This sometimes occurs because some in the group have enjoyed the *"democratic"* manner in which decisions are made, and they are reluctant to give up this power. We must be reminded that the church of Jesus Christ is not a democracy. God's way is to have elders and deacons. It is not an institution where every member has voting rights as to what it does or does not do.

Sometimes we find those who do not meet the qualifications to be elders, but who are recognized as *"unofficial"* leaders in the congregation, making the process of selecting elders difficult or next to impossible because they are not willing to relinquish their position.

Sadly, it also may be that the preacher is fearful of losing his position as a decision-maker, and is therefore not eager for elders to be appointed. For whatever reason, when a congregation has qualified men who are willing to serve, and the congregation refuses to appoint them, they are unorganized by their own choice, and that is not scriptural.

Four Categories

In regard to leadership, a congregation will generally fall into one of the following categories:
1. It may be *"scripturally organized"* with qualified elders and deacons.
2. It may be *"scripturally unorganized,"* having no qualified men in the congregation to serve.
3. It may *"unscripturally organized,"* for example, having a one-man eldership.
4. It may be *"unscripturally unorganized,"* having qualified

men who are willing to serve, but the congregation chooses not to install them. [2]

Plurality of Elders

In New Testament times each local congregation, when fully organized, had a plurality of elders to oversee the work and a plurality of deacons to assist the elders. There was no such thing as a single elder over a congregation, and there cannot be such today. In Acts 14:23 we read *"So when they had appointed elders (plural) in every church..."* Titus 1:5 states *"For this reason I left you in Crete, that you should set in order the things that are lacking and appoint elders (plural) in every city as I commanded you."* In Philippians 1:1 Paul addressed the letter *"To all the saints in Christ Jesus who are in Philippi, with the bishops (plural) and deacons."* In New Testament congregations, wherever an eldership existed, it was always composed of two or more elders. That is our pattern for today.

Qualifications

One must be selected for the eldership based on his compliance with the qualifications as set down by Paul in I Timothy 3:1-7 and Titus 1:5-11. In addition, I Peter 5:1-3 should be consulted. If one fails to meet these Biblical qualifications, he must not be selected. It is not scriptural to appoint a man to the eldership simply on the basis of his popularity, executive abilities, or standing in the community. The Lord set down the qualifications and they cannot be ignored.

Along this line, Jerry Moffitt stated, *"There has always been a problem (and it may be growing) that brethren and elders see the qualifications of an elder to be that of a successful businessman rather than a godly and spiritual Christian. It is as if elders are only a decision-making board of directors.*

This mind-set usually sees the health of the church in terms of numerical count, finances, or contribution, and a beautiful building. It is not a matter of truth, spirituality, conflict with evil, zeal, or holiness, but more a matter of busy work, social life, and keeping people happy." [3]

Some of the qualifications touch the man's personal character, others touch his family life, but all are directed toward his ability to lead. Some are negative qualifications while others are positive. Some can be possessed by degree while others are absolute. All are important.

We sometimes hear that the first qualification to be an elder is that he must have the desire to serve. I Timothy 3:1 says *"If a man desires the position of a bishop, he desires a good work."* Without question, a man should desire to serve the Lord in this capacity before he accepts the position. It is not likely that a man could properly function in the eldership if he is doing so against his will. However, the desiring does not seem to be a qualification in the same sense as the others. The statement rather appears to be a commendation for those who are willing to do the work of a bishop in the Lord's church.

1. "Blameless" (NKJV)
I Timothy 3:2, Titus 1:7

The NASB translates this as *"above reproach."* The conduct of the man who is to be an elder must be above reproach. Even if reproach, censure, or blame is hurled at him unfairly it will not stick because of the reputation that he has established. *"The Greek word from which this comes means 'one who cannot be laid hold upon,' that is, a man who has given evil men no occasion whatever to blame or censure him."* [4] He is known as a man of truthfulness and honesty.

2. "The Husband of One Wife" (NKJV)
I Timothy 3:2, Titus 1:6

The first thing that this qualification establishes is that the elder is to be a man. Women have an honorable place in the church, but it is not in the eldership. The second thing that we notice is that the elder cannot be a bachelor. He must be married. Thirdly, he cannot be married to more than one wife. Polygamy is an evil under the law of Christ, and obviously, the elder cannot be a polygamist. Besides polygamy, there is another way that a man can have more than one wife. Biblically, a marriage is not dissolved in God's sight except for two reasons. The first is death. The second is divorce on the grounds of adultery. Jesus said in Matthew 19:9 *"And I say to you, whoever divorces his wife, except for sexual immorality, and marries another, commits adultery."* Since the marriage relationship can only be dissolved by death, or divorce on the grounds of adultery, any man who divorces his wife for any other cause and marries again has more than one living wife in God's sight. He is therefore excluded from the eldership.

3. "Temperate" (NKJV), "Vigilant" (KJV)
I Timothy 3:2

Titus 1:8 says *"self controlled."* This requirement has to do with the relationship of an elder to his appetites and passions. It describes a man of will power and self-control. Proverbs 25:28 tells us *"Whoever has no rule over his own spirit is like a city broken down, without walls."* The elder controls his thoughts, speech, and deeds. He keeps his desires and appetites in restraint. The ASV, NKJV, NASB, and the NIV all translate I Tim. 3:2 as *"temperate."* The KJV uses the word *"vigilant."* The elder must be watchful in regard to his own conduct as well as for dangers to the congregation. Barnes writes, *"The word*

... means properly, sober, temperate, abstinent, especially in respect to wine; thus sober-minded, watchful, circumspect."[5]

4. "Sober Minded" (NKJV)
I Timothy 3:2, Titus 1:8

The KJV uses the word *"sober,"* the NASB *"prudent,"* while the RSV uses *"sensible."* *"The word translated 'sensible' (sophron) signifies discreet, humble minded and modest."*[6] *"Perhaps the word 'prudent' would come nearer to the meaning of the apostle than any single word that we have."*[7] An elder must be sensible, not mentally unbalanced. He must be able to give serious consideration to all questions that may arise, considering seriously the issues and meeting them conscientiously and intelligently.

5. "Of Good Behavior" (NKJV)
I Timothy 3:2

The Greek kosmios means *"orderly."* Barnes says *"The most correct rendering ... would be that he should be a gentleman. He should not be slovenly in his appearance, or rough and boorish in his manners."*[8] He should be the kind of person of whom we would not be ashamed because of his neglect of plain old-fashioned good manners. All else being equal, the man who is mannerly, courteous, and polite will be able to do more good with more people than the one who lacks these attributes.

6. "Hospitable" (NKJV)
I Timothy 3:2, Titus 1:8

Literally the elder is to be *"a lover of good men."* Good will, kindliness, and generosity in caring for others, and a desire to make others feel at ease marks the hospitable person. The man who does not like to associate with others, who does not, and will not, open his home to visitors and make them feel welcome, does not fit the qualification *"given to hospitality."* (KJV)

7. "Able to Teach"
I Timothy 3:2

Titus 1:9 elaborates on this qualification by saying, *"Holding fast the faithful word as he has been taught, that he may be able, by sound doctrine, both to exhort and convince those who contradict."* From the combination of I Timothy 3:2 and Titus 1:9-11 we learn these things:

First, the elder must be a man of the Word. He must know what to teach. In order to do this, he must have more than a casual acquaintance with the Scriptures. There is no excuse for an elder who does not make a serious effort to know his Bible. If he is not mentally capable of understanding the Bible, he has no business being an elder. If he is lazy and indifferent about studying the Word, he has no business being an elder.

Secondly, he must be a man who is *"Holding fast the faithful word."* Here is a man who is convicted, mature, and stable in his knowledge of the word. He is not one who is *"Tossed to and fro and carried about with every wind of doctrine"* (Ephesians 4:14).

Thirdly, the elder must know how to teach. An elder must be an example to the flock, but he cannot fulfill this qualification merely by being a good example. He must be *"Able to teach."* One might wonder to what extent must this ability be possessed. Paul clarifies this by saying that he must be able by sound doctrine to refute false teaching and to close the mouths of those who are teaching what they ought not teach.

"Some, in trying to make up for this deficiency in the eldership, try to have at least one man who can teach, and

others who can look after other matters. But we may as well try to eliminate any of the other qualities in an elder as that of teaching. If not, why not? The Bible says a man 'must be apt to teach.' It also says he 'must be the husband of one wife.' According to such reasoning, if one of the elders had one wife, it would not matter how many the others had. Such an idea is ridiculous, of course. So we conclude that each elder should have all the qualifications set forth in the Bible to as great a degree as we are able to find in men." [9]

A failure to observe the qualification of being able to teach may well result in false teachers taking over a congregation while the elders sit idly by, relying on their good examples.

8. "Not Given to Wine" (NKJV)
I Timothy 3:3, Titus 1:7

The man who is given to wine is prohibited from being an elder in the Lord's church. One would think it unnecessary that any Christian would have to be warned about the growing evil of drinking, much less, a man who is apparently mature enough to be considered for the eldership. Unfortunately, we live in a time when many moral standards of conduct are being challenged and set aside. A drinking elder would have a bad influence on others and would hinder the work of the church. Members of the church would either lose respect for him, or they would be influenced to follow his example, while many outsiders would see him as hypocritical. In any case, it is unthinkable that a congregation would appoint such a one to be a shepherd over the flock.

Robert R. Taylor offers these strong words on the subject. *"Without any fear of successful contradiction from any source I confidently contend that a man who imbibes alcoholic beverages is not fit for the eldership of God's church."* [10] Burton

Coffman said, *"... it should be remembered that wines of our times have ten times the alcoholic percentage of wines in that day; and that, even in those times, the people who wanted to set the proper example abstained from wine altogether."* [11]

The church certainly does not need leaders who lack the moral conviction to say *"no"* to drinking, social or otherwise.

9. "Not Violent" (NKJV)
I Timothy 3:3, Titus 1:7

The KJV says *"No striker,"* the NASB *"Not pugnacious."* An elder must not be one who hurls abusive language at others, or one who is likely to settle his differences with his fists. Barnes says, *"He must be peaceable, not a quarrelsome man. This is connected with the caution about the use of wine, probably, because that is commonly found to produce a spirit of contention and strife."* [12] The ASV has the marginal note *"not quarrelsome over wine."*

10. "Not Greedy for Money" (NKJV) I Timothy 3:3
"Not Fond of Sordid Gain" (NASB) Titus 1:7

One who is being considered for the eldership must not be one whose life and heart is centered on the accumulation of wealth. If an elder has an inordinate affection for money he could be absorbed in that pursuit to the neglect of spiritual matters.

In addition, if he is a covetous individual he might be strongly tempted to compromise moral and ethical standards in order to obtain money. This does not prohibit an elder from having money, even much money, but it does insist that he not place undue value on it.

Paul clearly lays out the danger of having an inordinate desire for money in I Timothy 6:9-10: *"But those who desire to be rich* fall into temptation and a snare, and into many foolish and harmful lusts which drown men in destruction and perdition. For the love of money is a root of all kinds of evil" (NKJV). This danger not only applies to those who would be elders, but to all Christians alike.

11. "Gentle" (NKJV)
I Timothy 3:3

The KJV uses the word *"patient."* Lipscomb says, *"Not bitter and impatient, but kind in manners even to the ... unpleasant."* [13] The elder is to be kind and have a pleasant disposition. *"The same word (epieike) is translated forbearance, or gentleness (Philippians 4:5, Col. 3:13) kindness or graciousness (Acts 24:14)."* [14]

12. "Not Quarrelsome" (NKJV)
I Timothy 3:3

The KJV says *"Not a brawler."* The ASV has *"Not contentious."* This qualification tells us that the elder is not to be a person who is disposed to fight and to be quarrelsome. This certainly does not mean that an elder should refuse to stand up and contend for the truth (Jude v. 3). This is part of his responsibility as a shepherd who protects the flock. However, even truth and right should not be maintained in a contentious spirit. He should avoid squabbling.

13. "One Who Rules Well His Own House" (NKJV)
I Timothy 3:4

Titus 1:6 adds, *"Having faithful children not accused of dissipation or insubordination."* The NASB says *"Having children who believe, not accused of dissipation or rebellion."*

Paul gives the reason for this qualification in I Timothy 3:5, *"For if a man does not know how to rule his own house, how will he take care of the church of God?"*

The elder is to be a family man, having believing children. *"Believing"* means that they are Christians, members of the Lord's church. Coffman states, *"The emphasis in this verse is not upon procreative ability, but upon the ability to rule, a well disciplined family being the surest evidence of such a trait in one considered for the eldership."* [15]

Unfortunately, too many men have been appointed to the eldership primarily on the basis that they have believing children. This in spite of the fact that they were ignorant of God's Word, were not able to teach, nor were they able to guard the flock against false teachers. Nevertheless, it is necessary for an elder to have a family. A bachelor could not qualify for the eldership, for he has not proven his leadership ability in the home.

14. "Not a Novice" (NKJV)
I Timothy 3:6

The NASB says, *"Not a new convert"* A *"novice"* is a new Christian or one with little experience in the Christian life. Without experience in Christian living and the maturity that it brings, he could not possibly assume and perform effectively the weighty responsibilities of the eldership. An elder must be a man who has proven himself and his loyalty to the Lord and His Word.

If a novice is appointed to this position, he is likely to become conceited or puffed up, and in that state becomes an easy prey for the devil. How long should a person be a member of the Lord's church before he can be an elder? We are not told. Some men develop more rapidly than others, while some never develop. The church should be able to determine when a man is sufficiently matured in the faith to accept this great responsibility.

15. "Must Have a Good Testimony Among Those Who Are Outside" (NKJV)
I Timothy 3:7

The NASB says, *"And he must have a good reputation with those outside the church."* The whole church is judged by its leaders. The elder must conduct himself so as to receive the respect of the community. It would create a most difficult situation for a man to be leading the flock who was considered by the community to be a scoundrel, thief, or a drunkard. Any good that the congregation could do would be nullified by this one man.

James D. Cox points out, *"If the church leader had lived a sub-standard life in recent years then those who knew him on the outside would soon snare him and return him to the snake pit. It takes time to overcome. It takes years after living promiscuously for the community to change their testimony of that old life."* [16]

16. "Not Self-Willed" (NKJV and NASB)
Titus 1:7

The elder is not to be self-pleasing, or self-willed. Rather, he is to be considerate of others. He is not to be arrogant in asserting his will to the congregation, or to the other elders. In matters of decision making regarding judgment or opinions, he is not to be a man who is unyielding. He should be ready to consider the wishes and desires of others in matters of opinion, realizing that no one elder has all wisdom. A self-willed, unyielding elder can destroy the peace of a congregation and hinder its progress. Such men should be avoided. In I Peter 5:3 the apostle gave this instruction to elders, *"Nor as being lords over those entrusted to you, but being examples to the flock."*

17. "Not Quick-Tempered" (NKJV and NASB)
Titus 1:7

The elder must be one who can restrain himself. He must not be a *"hot head"* but one who has control of his anger. The eldership is a place for cool minds and controlled emotions.

18. "A Lover of What Is Good" (NKJV)
"Loving What Is Good" (NASB)
Titus 1:8

A congregation should desire a man who will "Abhor what is evil. Cling to what is good" (Romans 12:9). His desires will not be for that which is wrong or questionable, but that which is good and pure.

19. "Just" (NKJV and NASB)
Titus 1:8

In the sense that the word just is used here, it has to do with the way the man deals with other people. The elder will have many decisions to make which will affect others. He will be called upon at times to judge between brethren, and in all his decisions he must be impartial and fair. He must be honest and ethical in his dealing with others.

21. "Holy" (NKJV)
Titus 1:8

The NASB uses the word *"devout."* The man who would be an elder must be deeply devoted to God. He must be God-fearing and righteous. It is God that we all must please. The elder, along with all other Christians, must strive to be a holy priesthood and a holy nation (I Peter 2:5,9). God is holy, and we are to make every effort to be like Him (I Peter 1:16).

Authority and Example

While some have suggested that elders have no authority, the Scriptures make it abundantly clear that such an assertion is in error. We are living in an age of permissiveness where authority in many areas is being rejected. However, the Word of God is too clear on this subject to be misunderstood. We must not make the mistake of rejecting the God-given authority that rightfully belongs to the eldership.

Those who would take the authority away from the elders say that he functions only by example. I Peter 5:3 is given as the proof-text. Without question, elders are to be examples of Christian living to the flock. Furthermore, they are not to be dictators. No godly elder would want to *"lord it over the flock."*

However, it is a serious mistake to jump to the conclusion that elders can only lead by example. Two verses earlier Peter said, **"Shepherd the flock of God which is among you, serving as overseers."** The shepherd must do more for his flock than be a good example. He must take the oversight. This includes feeding, directing, restoring, and disciplining. An overseer is one who has authority. The command to exercise the oversight was not given in verse two and then taken away in verse three when the elders were told to be examples. It is totally consistent with the text that elders are to have authority as well as the responsibility of being good examples to the congregation.

"Most church problems in recent years, including lack of growth, stem from an attitude on the part of leadership.

We have lost our place before the people because we have adopted a policy of leading by passive example only." [17]

Hebrews 13:17 should remove all doubt about elders having authority: *"Obey those who rule over you, and be submissive, for they watch out for your souls."* The words rule, obey, and submissive clearly place authority with the elders. Also, I Timothy 5:17 says, *"Let the elders who rule well be counted worthy of double honor."* Those who rule must have authority.

Another passage is Acts 20:28, in which Paul said to the elders of Ephesus, *"Take heed to yourselves and to all the flock, among which the Holy Spirit has made you overseers."* Again, we see the word that places authority with the elders.

The authority that resides in the eldership was given to them by the Lord who was given all authority in heaven and on earth (Matthew 28:18). It should be made clear that the authority of an eldership is not the same thing as the authority of an elder. *"Sometimes an elder will have the mistaken idea that he, as an individual elder, has some authority to make decisions with reference to the congregation. But the authority ... does not reside in an elder, but in an eldership."* [18] Of course one elder can be delegated by the body of elders to handle some particular job, but when he does so, he is acting on behalf of the eldership.

Duty of Elders to the Church

The elders of a church are to lead in all phases of the work, by deed as well as by word. They should be examples to the congregation in their faithful attendance to all the services and other activities of the congregation. Elders cannot oversee, feed, protect, correct, and encourage spiritual activity and growth when they absent themselves from the assembly of the saints. The elders express their interest in the programs of the church by their participation, and by their encouragement to the members to participate.

Elders watch out for the souls of those in the congregation as those who must give account (Hebrews 13:17). They need to know the flock and be willing to visit them, and to be involved with them in guidance, correction, and problem solving, as well as discipline.

Elders must guard the church against false teachers (Titus 1:9), and hold up the hands of faithful teachers and preachers as they teach sound doctrine. The apostle Paul warned, *"Also from among yourselves men will rise up, speaking perverse things, to draw the disciples after them"* (Acts 20:30).

Elders must watch for the weak in the church. Just as sheep have a tendency to wander away from the flock, weak members stray away from the church. Elders are spiritual shepherds who must watch over the flock, striving to return the wandering ones to the fold.

Elders must plan and direct the work of the church, never forgetting its purpose is to save souls. They are responsible to see that the congregation receives a balanced diet of Bible teaching that will cause them to grow in the Word, and to be fortified to stand against those who would draw them away from the truth. Elders have the responsibility for that which is taught from the pulpit. They also have the responsibility for that which is taught in the Bible classes. Preachers and Bible teachers alike work under the oversight of the elders.

Because of denominational influences, the role of the elder is sometimes confused with that of the preacher. We often hear people referring to the preacher as *"pastor."* Unless the preacher happens also to be an elder, he is not a *"pastor,"* and should not be addressed as such. The Elders are the *"pastors"* who shepherd the flock. The work of an eldership is a never ending task for they must constantly watch and care for the church, defending it against the forces of Satan.

Duty of the Church to the Elders

From the following passages we learn some of the duties that members have to the elders. It is apparent that some church members have absolutely no conception of the duty, regard, concern and respect which the Bible teaches them to have for an eldership. We are to recognize them and esteem them very highly in love for their work's sake (I Thessalonians 5:12-13).

We are to *"imitate the faith"* of the elders (Hebrews 13:7). Paul was able to say, *"Imitate me, just as I imitate Christ"* (I Corinthians 11:1). In like manner, we are to imitate the elders as they walk in righteousness. Members should be able to see what the elders do and be safe in following their examples.

We are to obey and be submissive to the elders (Hebrews 12:17). The elders cannot rule, guide, and watch over a congregation if the members persist in paying no attention to them.

Elders may be counted worthy of double honor (I Timothy 5:17). First, they should be honored for the worthy work that they do. We should honor them and hold them in high esteem for their willingness to serve in a work that is frequently a thankless task. We honor them because they have met the qualifications that permitted them to be appointed. We honor them because they feed us and tend to our spiritual needs. We honor them because they watch for our souls. We honor them because of the delegated authority the Lord has given them to rule over us. We honor them because of their knowledge of the Word and their dedication to it. Elders deserve our respect, our honor, and our cooperation. [19] They do not deserve our constant criticism, fault-finding, complaining, and bickering.

A second way that elders may be honored is by being financially supported by the congregation so that their full time can be devoted to the work. While this is not a very common practice, it is a scriptural concept and many congregations could benefit from such an arrangement.

An accusation against an elder is not to be received except it come from two or three witnesses (I Timothy 5:19). Unkind and unfair things may be said about a godly man by a mean-spirited individual who is motivated by jealousy or resentment. Such must be rejected unless there are two or three witnesses of the alleged evil.

Autonomy and the Elders

The authority of an eldership does not extend beyond the congregation that it serves. It doesn't matter how large a congregation is or how strong it is, it has no authority over another congregation regardless how small or how weak that congregation happens to be. Love and cooperation should exist between all faithful congregations, but that does not extend to a governmental arrangement where one congregation is under the authority of another.

How to Appoint Elders

The Scriptures do not give us an exact pattern for selecting elders. Therefore, it is left up to us to select a method that results in qualified men being appointed in an orderly manner. In Acts 6, when seven special servants were chosen, the apostles had the disciples do the selecting from among themselves. In the absence of specific instructions, this principle can be applied equally well in the selecting of elders. The following is offered only as a suggestion, and applies only where there are no existing elders.

To begin the process, the preacher should preach a series of lessons on the subject of elders. At the same time, classes conducted on the subject would be helpful. The congregation should be encouraged to study the matter carefully. Care should be given in the teaching that the congregation make a distinction between scriptural objections and those that are trivial. A group of men should be appointed to handle the process.

The congregation should be asked to submit the names of those men whom they feel are qualified. To accomplish this, a form should be given to each member. This would include a list of the qualifications from I Timothy 3 and Titus 1, blank spaces for the suggested names, and a place for the signature of the one submitting the names. About two weeks should be allowed for the names to be submitted.

At the end of that period, those receiving a reasonable number of suggestions would be contacted by the committee to see if they are interested in serving. Those who agree to serve then have their names placed before the congregation. The congregation is asked to consider those men, and submit any scriptural reasons why any of them should not serve. It is best to have those objections put in writing and signed by the one who does the objecting. Allow about two weeks for this procedure. At the end of that time, the men who remain in the process would be placed before the congregation as elders. While this procedure gives a simple framework for the process, congregations may wish to make variations or elaborate on the details. Any method, as long as it does not violate Scripture, should be appropriate.

Elders Must Stand Together

Ideally, every decision an eldership makes should be unanimous. However, this does not always happen. Therefore, we suggest that it should be the agreement of each eldership that the majority of those present in their meetings will carry a decision. Even though there may not have been full agreement on a matter, the elders should present a unified position to the congregation. *"An elder should not be guilty of making even the most casual remark of having been for something, but over-ruled in the decision made because the other elders were against it. Defend the decisions you make at the right time and in the right place -- the meeting of your eldership -- forever after holding your tongue and peace."* [20] Using poor judgment in this matter, perhaps in an effort to gain favor with an element in the congregation, is a very serious matter. It could result in division.

Conclusion

When a man becomes a part of an eldership he takes on responsibilities, cares, and anxieties for the church. Unfortunately, he may not always be treated fairly and respectfully. He may be subjected at times to unfair criticism. However, there are also many rewards, such as the joy of service, and the knowledge that the church has benefited by his work of love. There is the feeling of accomplishment that problems have been faced and solved rightfully. There is great joy in associating closely with the best people on the face of the earth. Indeed, there is deep satisfaction in knowing that he is doing a work that was ordained by God Himself.

Footnotes

1. J.W. McGarvey, A Treatise on the Eldership, DeHoff Publications, Murfreesboro, TN, p. 21.
2. James D. Cox, With the Bishops and Deacons, Published by Author, Tustin, California, pp. 304-305

3. Jerry Moffitt, Leadership, 1997 Bellview Lectures, "Elders and the Stewardship of Souls," Bellview Church of Christ, Pensacola, Florida, p. 175.
4. James Burton Coffman, Commentary on I and II Timothy, Firm Foundation Pub. House, Austin, Texas, p. 175.
5. Albert Barnes, Barnes Notes, Kregel Publications, Grand Rapids, Michigan, p. 1139.
6. Carl Spain, Letters of Paul to Timothy and Titus, Living Word Comm., R.B. Sweet and Co., Austin, Texas, p. 57.
7. Barnes, p. 1139.
8. Ibid., p. 1139.
9. R.W. Grimsley, The Church and its Elders, Quality Printing Co., Inc., Abilene, Texas, pp. 49-50.
10. Robert R. Taylor, The Elder and His Work, Taylor Publications, Ripley, Tennessee, p. 89.
11. Coffman, p. 177.
12. Barnes, p. 1139.
13. David Lipscomb, Commentary on the New Testament Epistles, Gospel Advocate, Nashville, Tennessee, p. 147.
14. Spain, p. 59.
15. Coffman, p. 179.
16. Cox, p. 47
17. Cox, p. 239.
18. Bobby Duncan, Leadership, 1997 Bellview Lectures, "Authority of Elders," Bellview Church of Christ, Pensacola, Florida, p. 28.
19. Taylor, p. 207.
20. Cleon Lyles, Bigger Men For Better Churches, Published by author, Little Rock, Arkansas, p. 25.

CHAPTER 14
IS CHURCH ATTENDANCE NECESSARY?

A Most Unusual Funeral

The story is told about a preacher conducting a funeral service for church members who failed to attend the assemblies of the church. He reasoned that since these were not alive and active, they must be dead and therefore should have the benefit of a funeral. He placed the names of several *"dead"* members in a small artificial casket. The *"funeral"* was held on Sunday evening. Some of the names were:

Miss Lotta Services,
I Wanna Stayhome,
Illa Comeback Someday,
I.B. Bored,
Dan Ratherbe Elsewhere,
I.M. Luke Warm,
Phil Mypew Formee,
Ima Inna Badmood

Obviously, this *"funeral"* never really happened, but if such did take place how many of us would be represented in that *"casket"*?

God Is Concerned

While many church members today apparently think it is of little importance to attend the church services, we need to be reminded that God has always been concerned with the assembling of his people together for worship. Long before the Lord's church came into existence, the duty of assembling was an important practice during the Mosaic period. The Lord even ordained two silver trumpets to call the people together (Num. 10:2-3). The attitude of faithful Jews was expressed by the Psalmist when he said, *"I was glad when they said unto me, let us go into the house of the Lord"* (Psalms 122:1 NKJV).

Good, but Not Necessary?

Some today seem to believe that it is good to attend, but if there is something else of interest to do, church attendance is of lessor importance. The fact of the matter is, it is not only good to assemble, it is sinful not to do so. Clearly, the Lord considered assembling together for worship and fellowship as a vital part of the Christian's life. It was important enough to the Lord that he commanded Christians to meet regularly to engage in worship: *"Not forsaking the assembling of ourselves together, as the manner of some, but exhorting one another, and so much the more as you see the day approaching"* (Hebrews 10:25).

The Early Church Assembled

The practice of the early church meeting on the first day of the week was recorded in Acts 20:7. This set before Christians of all ages the inspired example that is imitated by the faithful today. *"Now on the first day of the week, when the disciples came together to break bread, Paul, ready to depart the next day,* spoke to them and continued his message until midnight."

The church of Christ at Corinth met on the first day of the week. They were to use this regular day of meeting to contribute of their means: *"On the first day of the week let each one of you lay something aside, storing up as he may prosper, that there be no collections when I come"* (I Corinthians 16:2).

Christians who desire to please the Lord must still assemble on Sunday to worship Him. It was on this special day that Jesus arose victoriously from the grave. It was on Sunday that Jesus appeared to His disciples before ascending into heaven. It was on Sunday that the church of Christ was established. It was on Sunday that the Holy Spirit was given to the apostles to guide them into all truth. It was on Sunday that the disciples of the first century observed the Lord's Supper.

Only on Sunday?

But, what about our attendance to assemblies that occur on days other than the Lord's day? The early church certainly did not limit their assembling together just on Sunday. Consider the following: All of those who were converted on the day of Pentecost in Jerusalem were together and had all things in common (Acts 2:44). Later, the disciples met and prayed together (Acts 4:31). Still later, Peter, having been released from prison, went to the home of John Mark and his mother Mary where many had assembled together for prayer (Acts 12:12).

Barnabus took Saul (Paul) to Antioch where they met with the church for an entire year and many were taught (Acts 11:26). When Paul and Barnabus returned from a missionary journey they gathered the church together and reported to them all the things that God had done through them (Acts 14:27). At Corinth the church gathered together for the purpose of disciplining a wayward member (I Corinthians 5:4).

It is not reasonable to conclude that all of these assemblies took place on the Lord's day. Those who might conclude such should be reminded of Acts 2:46 that states *"So continuing daily with one accord in the temple, and breaking bread from house to house, they ate their food with gladness and simplicity of heart."* When we think of the many assemblies the early church had, the direct command that they were not to miss assembling together takes on more meaning than just the Sunday morning worship.

Hindrance from God?

The only hindrance that should keep one from the assembly is a hindrance from God. If we are ill or otherwise hindered by the Lord, He does not expect us to assemble. However, the truth of the matter is that we often stretch an excuse to such an extreme that we create a hindrance and say it is from God. Parents may run around with their children all day long on Wednesday, but when evening comes the *"children are just too tired to go to Bible study."*

Sometimes secular work is done at the time of church meetings when it could just as easily be done at other times. Or, sometimes we knowingly schedule ourselves for non-essential activities that will regularly keep us away from church assemblies on Sunday night or Wednesday evenings. Have we ever considered how insulting to the Lord it must be for us to feel well enough to go anywhere and do anything, except to meet with the brethren?

Seek First the Kingdom

It is a strong congregation whose members can be counted upon to assemble together unless they are truly hindered from the Lord.

The principle that Jesus stated in Matt. 6:33 to *"But seek first the kingdom of God and His righteousness, and all these things shall be added to you."* Seeking first the kingdom of God is the basis that faithful Christians should use in determining whether or not to assemble with the church. Placing the Lord's church before the other things that compete for our time and energy is certainly the proper attitude.

The Lord in Our Midst

If we believe Matthew 18:20 *"For where two or three are gathered together in my name, I am there in the midst of them,"* we will then realize that if we absent ourselves from the assembly, we remove ourselves from a meeting where the Lord is present.

We Miss Instruction

When one misses the assembly he not only misses meeting with the Lord, he also misses the receiving of valuable instruction. Since he is not there, he will not be edified with the rest of the saints (I Corinthians 14:12.) Who among us is so filled with information and wisdom that we have no need for further study, or a need to be built up in the faith?

The Christian life is one of constant growth (2 Pet. 1:5-7). One may learn something from every lesson taught, or at least be reminded of great Bible truths. How often a spiritual lesson is taught, but many who need to hear it have chosen to stay home, go fishing, play golf, or be elsewhere. Building a strong congregation is the work of every member. A strong church cannot be built by a weak membership. It is difficult to build strong Christian character by erratic attendance.

We Miss Communication

When one does not attend all the services of the church he also misses communication with other Christians. Some members feel like *"outsiders"* because they never seem to know what is going on in the congregation. The reason for this is quite simple. They fail to attend the assemblies where congregational news is given.

We Miss Associating with Other Christians

When one does not attend the various assemblies he also misses associating with other Christians. We all need the association of brothers and sisters in Christ so that we can encourage others as well as be encouraged. We need to comfort others as well as be comforted. *"And let us consider one another in order to stir up love and good works"* (Hebrews 10:24).

Just a Private Matter?

Attendance is not just a *"private matter"* as some would like to think. Other Christians are looking at us, and they are affected by our examples. It is a very serious matter when a poor example is set before a weak brother or sister. A poor example in the matter of attendance might well set a new or weak member on the road to a complete falling away. Jesus had much to say about the influence of Christians on others. *"But you are the salt of the earth; but if the salt loses its flavor, how shall it be seasoned? It is then good for nothing but to be thrown out and trampled underfoot by men"* (Matt. 5:13). Not only are Christians to be the salt of the earth, but they are also to be the light of the world. *"You are the light of the world. A city that is set on a hill cannot be hidden.*

Nor do they light a lamp and put it under a basket, but on a lampstand, and it gives light to all who are in the house. Let your light so shine before men, that they may see your good works and glorify your Father in heaven" (Matt. 5:14-16).

Our own children are being told by our pattern of attendance what we consider important and what we consider unimportant. If we allow the smallest thing to keep us away from the assemblies, surely we are giving a message that is loud and clear to our children. The attitude of the parent will likely become the attitude of the child. Camping, fishing trips and recreational activities are good and beneficial, but surely they can be arranged so that the Lord will not be neglected.

Encourage Each Other to Attend

We can become stronger individual Christians, and we can become stronger congregations if we will all become faithful attenders of all the assemblies. The exhortation of the Hebrew writer is just as applicable for us today as it was for the church of Christ over nineteen centuries ago: *"And let us consider one another in order to stir up love and good works, not forsaking the assembling of ourselves together, as is the manner of some, but exhorting one another, and so much the more, as you see the day approaching"* (Hebrews 10:24-25).

CHAPTER 15
THE LORD'S SUPPER: WHEN SHOULD WE OBSERVE IT?

When should we observe the Lord's Supper? Some churches observe it once each year, while others observe it semi-annually or quarterly. Some observe it on special occasions when they consider it appropriate. Still others observe the Lord's Supper every Sunday, fifty-two times per year. Who is right? How can we know what is correct?

Authority for What We Do

In the New Testament we find authority for the things that we do and teach in the Lord's church by Direct Command, Approved Example, and Necessary Inference. If we are going to have Bible authority for determining when to partake of the Lord's Supper, it will be found in one or more of these three areas.

An example of a Direct Command regarding the Lord's Supper is found in Matthew 26:26-27. When Jesus instituted this memorial, He took the bread and instructed *"Take eat; this is My Body"* (NKJV). Of the fruit of the vine He ordered *"Drink from it, all of you."*

Concerning the assembly of the church we also have a direct command: *"not forsaking the assembling of ourselves together, as is the manner of some, but exhorting one another, and so much the more as you see the Day approaching"* (Heb. 10:25).

In this passage we are told by Direct Command to not forsake the assembly. However, the Hebrew writer did not specify what the day of worship was. This was not necessary for Christians of the first century for they knew very well that the special day of worship was the Lord's Day, the first day of the week. We can quickly verify this by an Approved Example found in Acts 20:7. *"Now on the first day of the week, when the disciples came together to break bread, Paul, ready to depart the next day, spoke to them and continued his message until midnight."*

The Early Christians Met on the First Day to "Break Bread"

Acts 20:7 contains a clear reference to the weekly observance of the Lord's Supper. This is an authoritative example for the church to follow as long as time will last. The purpose of the weekly assembly of the church was *"to break bread,"* meaning to observe the Lord's Supper, to remember Jesus in the manner He had instructed.

Obviously, it was the practice of the first century Christians to meet for worship on the first day of the week, Sunday. This was the Lord's Day. It was the day that Jesus arose from the grave. It was the day the church was established. It was incidental that Paul happened to be there and preached to them. With, or without Paul, these disciples met each Sunday for worship, and that worship included the Lord's Supper. This is a Holy Spirit Approved Example for us. We need no more than this to substantiate that we are to do the same thing today.

One Approved Example Is Enough

It is true that Acts 20:7 is the only verse in the New Testament which specifically states the day on which Christians met to commune, but this verse has sufficient information within itself to answer the question **"When should we partake of the Lord's Supper?"** The first day of the week was the day the first century Christians assembled for worship. It is not reasonable to conclude that these Christians met fifty-two times each year to remember the resurrection, but only once or twice to commemorate His death.

They Contributed on the First Day

When Paul wrote to the church at Corinth he designated that collections or contributions should be taken up on the first day of the week: **"Now concerning the collection for the saints, as I have given orders to the churches of Galatia, so you must do also: On the first day of the week as he may prosper, that there be no collections when I come."** (I Cor. 16:1-2).

Paul had given the same orders about the collections to the churches of Galatia. Meeting on the first day of the week for worship and observance of the Lord's Supper was a well-established practice by this time. Since the Christians were already meeting on the first day of the week Paul gave the Direct Command regarding the collection to coincide with their regular meeting.

What Pleases the Lord?

Whenever an effort is made to determine the proper day on which to observe the Lord's Supper, it must be determined on the basis of what pleases the Lord, and not what pleases us or makes us feel good.

Which Sabbath Did the Jews Observe?

Someone might suggest that there is no indication in Acts 20:7 that they came together every first day of the week. There is a parallel case under the Law of Moses that will help us to reach the correct conclusion in this matter. In the Old Testament, the Jews received the Ten Commandments. The fourth commandment stated, *"Remember the Sabbath day, to keep it holy"* (Exodus 20:8). Please notice that this does not say every Sabbath day, but it could mean nothing else. Every week included a seventh day or Sabbath, and every faithful Jew kept that day holy under the Law of Moses.

Likewise in the Christian dispensation, in the cycle of every seven days there comes a first day of the week. This is the *"Lord's Day,"* and Christians are to *"break bread"* upon this day. The regularity of this observance should be no more a question for the Christian than the observance of the Sabbath was for the Jew under the Law of Moses.

Which 4th of July?

Every year our nation sets aside a holiday that is dedicated to celebrating our independence. That day is always the same, the fourth of July. You would consider it a strange question if someone were to ask, *"On which fourth of July do you celebrate the country's independence?"* You would answer, *"<u>Every</u> fourth of July, of course."* Our independence is celebrated every time there is a fourth of July, and there is one every year. In Acts 20:7 it is obvious that the early church met on each and every Lord's Day, Sunday, to observe the Lord's Supper.

We Have Authority for the First Day of the Week

Please note that we have a Direct Command for taking the Lord's Supper. (Matt. 26:26-27). We have a Direct Command for attending the assembly (Heb. 10:25). We have a Direct Command for giving of our means on the first day of the week (I Cor. 16:1-2). We have an Approved Example for meeting on Sunday to observe the Lord's Supper (Acts 20:7). Since the practice of the early church was to meet on the first day of the week, and every week has a first day, by Necessary Inference we conclude that the church of the first century observed the Lord's Supper <u>every week</u> on the first day, Sunday.

Will It Lose its Meaning?

Some are very quick to argue that the Lord's Supper will become routine and meaningless to us if we take of it every week. Therefore, they argue, we should only observe this memorial once or twice per year? On the surface that might sound reasonable to one who is not well acquainted with God's Word. However, on the same basis could we not also argue that we should not meet for worship on a weekly basis? After all, assembling could become routine and meaningless to us.

Prayer is a wonderful thing. We don't want it to become meaningless, so could we not also argue that we should only pray once or twice per year? Singing to God could also become routine and meaningless. Using the same argument should we only sing to God once or twice each year? Even the most naive could not accept this logic when it comes to assembling, praying, and singing, but they fall into the trap of trying to out-think God when it comes to the Lord's Supper.

The Responsibility Is Ours

If we observe the Lord's Supper properly each week as a memorial, with each person examining himself as instructed (I Cor. 11:28), the Lord's Supper will not become meaningless. This is so important that Paul warned the Corinthians that if they did not observe the communion in a proper manner they would become guilty of the body and blood of Jesus. It is the responsibility of each one of us who participates in the Lord's Supper to not allow it to become routine and common place.

Can We Improve on God's Way?

I cannot think of one single case where man has ever improved on the Lord's way. Determining when to partake of the Lord's Supper is certainly no exception. Wouldn't it make more sense to show faith and trust in the Lord and let him have His way? Every faithful child of God should not only be willing, but eager to meet with the Lord's people <u>every</u> Sunday to partake of that memorial feast that so fittingly represents our Lord who was crucified on the cross so that we might have life eternal.

CHAPTER 16
WHAT ABOUT THE LORD'S SUPPER AND THE ONE CUP ISSUE?

Our hearts are saddened at the needless number of divisions that exist in the Lord's church. Some of the causes of these divisions may seem insignificant to us, but they are not insignificant if division is the result of their being accepted and taught. One such doctrine dictates that when the Lord's Supper is served the entire congregation must drink from one cup. If the New Testament required this of Christians, then we would all plead for its acceptance. However, the New Testament does NOT teach this. We have no right to demand that any congregation follow this teaching. I have been in Africa and have seen first hand where congregations have been divided or destroyed over this peculiar doctrine. The same thing has occurred in other parts of the world.

The New Testament Condemns Division

The apostle Paul condemned division in no uncertain words in I Corinthians 1:10: *"Now I plead with you, brethren, by the name of our Lord Jesus Christ, that you all speak the same thing, and that there be no divisions among you, but that you be perfectly joined together in the same mind and in the same judgment."* (NKJV)

Christ prayed for the unity of His followers: *"I do not pray for these alone, but also for those who will believe in Me through their word; that they all may be one, as You, Father, are in Me, and I in You; that the world may believe that You sent Me."* (John 17:20-21)

The cause of Christ suffers when brethren get tangled up with man-made restrictions and burdens, and bind them on the brotherhood. This is exactly what the *"one cup"* issue is. The Lord did not bind upon His followers the practice of using only one container when drinking the fruit of the vine in observance of the Lord's Supper. For any man to bind such a practice upon the body of Christ can only result in harm to the church and its effectiveness to those outside the body.

This chapter is written with the plea that, as brethren, we unite upon the Word of God and not allow Satan to divide us over false positions that some well-meaning brethren have taken.

When Jesus Instituted the Lord's Supper, He Used Figurative Language

The fact that the Lord used figurative language regarding the Lord's Supper cannot be denied. Please observe I Corinthians 11:24-27:

"For I received from the Lord that which I also delivered to you: that the Lord Jesus on the same night in which He was betrayed took bread; and when He had given thanks, He broke it and said, 'Take eat; THIS IS MY BODY which is broken for you; do this in remembrance of Me.' In the same manner He also took the cup after supper, saying, 'THIS CUP IS THE NEW COVENANT IN MY BLOOD. This do, as often as you drink it, in remembrance of Me. For as often as you eat this bread and DRINK THIS CUP, you proclaim the Lord's death till He comes. Therefore whoever eats this bread or DRINKS THIS CUP of the Lord in an unworthy manner will be guilty of the body and blood of the Lord.'"

Even though Jesus said *"This is my body,"* we understand that this is figurative language meaning *"this represents My body."* The bread is not the actual body of Jesus. It is symbolic of His body. When He said *"This cup is the new covenant in My blood,"* we understand that Jesus did not mean that He was literally holding the written law of God in His hand. When He said that those who drink of the cup in an unworthy manner *"Will be guilty of the body and blood of the Lord,"* we understand that He did not mean that we were the actual individuals who nailed Jesus to the cross, nor did we actually pierce His side. Obviously, the Lord was using figurative language.

It is interesting to note that when the *"one cup"* advocates look at all the passages pertaining to the Lord's Supper, they see only *"The cup"* as literal, but *"My body"* and *"My blood"* they see as figurative.

The Account by Matthew

The events that took place when Jesus instituted the Lord's Supper were recorded by Matthew as follows:

And as they were eating, Jesus took bread, blessed and broke it, and gave it to the disciples and said, *"Take, eat; THIS IS MY BODY."* Then He took the cup, and gave thanks, and gave it to them, saying *"Drink from it, all of you. For THIS IS MY BLOOD of the new covenant, which is shed for many for the remission of sins. But I say to you, I will not drink of this FRUIT OF THE VINE from now on until that day when I drink it new with you in My Father's kingdom."* (Matt. 26:26-29)

Clearly, figurative language is used by the Master. The bread is representative of the body, and the cup, or fruit of the vine, is representative of the blood of Jesus.

The Account by Mark

In Mark 14:22-25 the events are recorded in these words:
"And as they were eating, Jesus took bread, blessed and broke it, and gave it to them and said, 'Take, eat; THIS IS MY BODY.' Then He took the cup, and when He had given thanks He gave it to them, and they all drank from it. And He said to them, 'THIS IS MY BLOOD of the new covenant, which is shed for many. Assuredly, I say to you, I will no longer drink of the FRUIT OF THE VINE until that day when I drink it new in the kingdom of God.'"

It could not be clearer that figurative language is used here with the bread representing the body and the cup, the fruit of the vine, representing the blood. Luke also records these events in Luke 22:17-20.

Consider the Cup As a Figure

Actually, the cup is a double figure. The cup is made to stand for the fruit of the vine, which itself is symbolic of the blood of Jesus. The reader must not lose sight of the purpose of the Lord's Supper. It was then, and still is, a memorial of the body and blood of Jesus. It points us back to the death of Christ on the cross.

Jesus used the expression *"the cup"* when He was emphasizing the contents of the cup. The container is not in any way a fitting symbol of the blood of Jesus. The contents, the fruit of the vine, is a fitting symbol of the blood of Jesus.

The Use of Metonymy

When Jesus referred to the fruit of the vine as *"the cup"* He was utilizing the figure of speech which we know as metonymy.

"**Metonymy**" is defined as: "*The use of the name of one thing in place of the name of something it symbolizes, i.e. 'crown' for 'king.'*" (The New Lexicon Webster's Dictionary) This figure is often used in the Bible. Consider the following examples: In Luke 16:29 it says, "*They have Moses and the Prophets.*" What is obviously meant here is that they have the writings of Moses and the prophets. One word is allowed to stand for another. In Genesis 6:11 it states that "*The earth was corrupt.*" Actually, the people were corrupt. The word "**earth**" stands for the word "**people.**" In John 3:16 we read that "*God so loved the world.*" We all understand that he loved the people of the world. The word "**world**" is the metonymy which stands for the word "**people.**"

It is easy to understand in the examples above how the figure of speech works. Is it not equally easy to see that when Jesus used the word "**cup**" He was allowing it to stand for "*the fruit of the vine?*" This is made abundantly clear when we look at the words of Jesus: "*Drink from it (cup) all of you*"...."*I will not drink of the fruit of the vine from now on...*" (Matt. 26:26-29) "*Then He took the cup ....this is My blood*".... "*I will no longer drink of the fruit of the vine until that day when I drink it new in the kingdom of God.*" (Mark 14:22-25) Likewise He also took the cup after supper, saying "*This cup is the new covenant...*" (Luke 22:20)

Reasons Why One Cup Is Not Mandatory

Those who contend that it is mandatory to use only ONE container in observing the Lord's Supper point out that Jesus took "the" cup or "a" cup. Therefore, they declare, when we use more than one container in taking of the fruit of the vine, we sin. Please observe several reasons why it is NOT mandatory to use ONE container in observing the Lord's Supper:

First: It Cannot Be Proved That the Apostles All Drank from One Vessel

On the contrary, we have reason to assume that the disciples divided the contents of the cup that Jesus passed just as they did with the earlier Passover cup of Luke 22:17. Of that earlier cup our Lord told the apostles, *"Take this and divide it among yourselves."*

If a man brings in a pitcher of cold water to a group of thirsty men and says to them, *"Here, share this among yourselves,"* would you expect for all to put their lips to the pitcher or would each be able to pour some in his own glass? Obviously, the latter is correct. In Luke 22:17 the most natural meaning of the words is that each poured some into his own vessel. The same seems to be indicated also in the *"cup"* of the Lord's Supper itself. The NASB renders the statement: *"This cup which is poured out for you is the new covenant in My blood"* (Luke 22:20).

Second: The Fact That the Disciples All Drank "From It" Doesn't Have to Mean That They All Put Their Lips to One Vessel

In John 4:12 we have the identical expression used concerning Jacob's Well. The Samaritan woman said that Jacob and his sons and his cattle all drank *"of it"*. Who would believe that all of them actually put their heads down into the well itself and lapped the water from it? The expression *"of it"* refers to the source, regardless of how many containers were used.

Third: When Paul Said That We "Drink the Cup" in I Corinthians 11:26, He Had to Be Referring to Liquid, Not a Container

It is impossible to drink the container. The word *"cup"* here obviously stands for the contents, the fruit of the vine. *"Drink the cup"* does not bind the single container any more than the figurative reference to *"the cup"* in Matthew 20:22-23 means that Jesus and James and John were all going to die on the same cross or at the same time. *"But Jesus answered and said, ' you do not know what you ask. Are you able to drink the cup that I am about to drink?'......They said 'We are able.' He said to them 'You will indeed drink My cup.'"*

Jesus, James and John all drank of the cup of suffering, but they did not all suffer and die at the same time or even in the same way. The *"one cup"* advocates would immediately respond by saying that this is figurative language. Indeed, it is, and so is *"the cup"* of the Lord's Supper.

Please look at Mark 9:41 where reference is made to *"a cup"*. *"For whoever gives you a cup of water to drink in My name .... will by no means lose his reward."* If this compassionate person gives two cups of water, should we conclude that he will lose his reward? Of course not! No one would draw such a conclusion. Why then do we take the fact that Jesus took *"the cup"* and somehow arrive at the conclusion that we must *"drink the cup"* out of only one container?

Fourth: "The Cup" No More Requires One Container Than "The Fruit of the Vine" Requires One Grapevine

Paul's reference to *"one cup"* is to the liquid contents, not to one container. Wouldn't it be just as reasonable to require that the grape juice used in the Lord's Supper all come from ONE grapevine? After all, the record does say *"the vine."* No one would be so foolish as to insist on such a requirement.

Fifth: To Be Consistent With the "One Cup" Position, There Could Only Be One Container for All the Christians in All the World

The minute you have a second container for a sister congregation, you have more cups than Jesus held in His hand the night the Lord's Supper was instituted. The advocates of the *"one cup only"* position are obligated to answer this argument or their whole position falls immediately, even if all else is ignored. How could it be possible for all the congregations in existence to drink from one container? It is ridiculous to even consider such a possibility. The Lord never intended for us to have to wrestle with such a problem because He never made the use of one container a mandatory requirement for His people.

It is most improbable that the 3,000 that were converted on the day of Pentecost in Acts chapter 2 all drank from a single container when they observed the Lord's Supper. If they did, it would have been an extremely large cup, or else they would have had to refill the cup over and over again. If they filled the container a second time or a third time or a thousand times, was it still the same cup? Later on we read in Acts 4:4 that *"The number of men came to be about five thousand."* Is it reasonable to think that all 5000 drank from a single container when they participated in the Lord's Supper? Today, if 50,000 Christians gathered for worship on the Lord's Day, would the *"one cup"* advocates still insist on all 50,000 drinking from one container?

Sixth: Those Who Take Literally the Statement "Drink the Cup" Are Obligated to Consume the Container

Since those who advocate a single container in the Lord's Supper maintain that *"the cup"* is the container, for the twelve disciples to obey the Lord and "drink the cup," each of the disciples would have had to consume one-twelfth of the container! Having consumed the container, it would no longer be in existence for anyone else to *"drink it"*. While this creates a humorous picture, it does point out the fallacy of taking the position that *"the cup"* means the literal container.

Seventh: The Original Cup Would Need to Be Used

If one insists that *"the cup"* of which Jesus was speaking was the literal container, then the ORIGINAL cup that Jesus held in His hand is THE cup, and therefore, the only one that can be used. Any cup other than the one original cup is not THE cup.

Eighth: There Is No Virtue in Using a Single Container

When a congregation of God's people observe the Lord's Supper by using multiple containers, they have not altered the memorial service in any way. They still drink the fruit of the vine which is symbolic of the shed blood of Jesus. Likewise, those who use one container are also drinking of the fruit of the vine which is symbolic of the Lord's blood. Using one container does not do anything to enhance the Lord's Supper. Both accomplish exactly the same purpose.

How Many Elements in the Lord's Supper?

A few of those who advocate the *"one cup"* have taken a most unusual position in regard to the number of elements in the Lord's Supper. They contend that there are three (3) elements: the BREAD representing the BODY; the FRUIT OF THE VINE representing the BLOOD; and the CUP (CONTAINER) representing the NEW TESTAMENT. The addition of the CONTAINER as the third element in the Lord's Supper is absolutely without foundation, and at best must be termed a foolish position. Look at 1 Corinthians. 11:26-27. *"For as often as you eat this bread and drink this cup you proclaim the Lord's death till He comes. Therefore whoever eats this bread or drinks this cup of the Lord in an unworthy manner will be guilty of the body and blood of the Lord."* There is no way that one can drink a container. We can only drink the contents. Therefore, the container cannot possibly be meant here. Paul makes reference only to two elements in the Lord's Supper, namely *"eat this bread"* and *"drink this cup."* If one does not observe the Lord's Supper properly, he is guilty of the body and the blood of the Lord. He is certainly not guilty regarding the *"container of the Lord."* There are only two elements in the Lord's Supper, the bread and the fruit of the vine (the cup).

What about the Bread?

Those who concern themselves with the number of cups often forget about the bread. In I Corinthians 10:16 Paul said, *"The bread which we break, is it not the communion of the body of Christ?"* Doesn't the language *"the bread"* sound like the language of *"the cup"*? Those who want to divide the church over the use of one container for the fruit of the vine should see the inconsistency in their position of the number of loaves required in the Lord's Supper. Since they came to the conclusion that only one cup can be used because it says *"the cup,"* should they not also conclude that only one loaf of bread can be used because it says *"the bread?"* Is not *"the bread"* equally important with *"the cup?"* With a closer observation of I Corinthians 10:16 you will see that the *"we"* refers to the Ephesian Christians and the Corinthian Christians. They *"broke bread"* together even though they were miles apart. Obviously, *"the bread"* did not mean one loaf. To argue for one loaf is as foolish as arguing for one container in which to serve the fruit of the vine.

Can the bread be served on a plate? Ordinarily, that is the way that it is served today. However, it is not likely that Jesus served the bread on a plate. Will one be condemned for putting the bread on a plate? Of course not! Christ's disciples observed the Lord's Supper in an upper room. Must we do the same? Of course not! Will we be condemned for serving the fruit of the vine in more than one container? Of course not! What has any of this to do with the Lord's Supper being a memorial? ABSOLUTELY NOTHING! Our concentration should not be on containers, but on the crucified Christ!

We do great damage to the meaning of these passages pertaining to the cup of the Lord's Supper when we emphasize the container as being the focal point of Jesus' words. Jesus was not talking about containers. He was talking about the *"fruit of the vine,"* which was to be a memorial of His blood to be shed on the cross. *"This do, as often as you drink it, in remembrance of Me."*

For over 1900 years the followers of Christ have observed the Lord's Supper. In doing so, they have had their minds effectively called back to Calvary. There they have viewed the crucified Christ, the only begotten Son of God, as He shed His precious blood for the sins of the world. As long as time will last, faithful Christians will continue to observe this beautiful memorial feast.

CHAPTER 17
WHEN IS THE SECOND COMING OF CHRIST?

The Scriptures clearly teach that Christ is coming again. The New Testament abounds in passages about the Second Coming of Jesus. In fact, someone has counted more than three hundred passages that either mention or allude to that great event. While we might wonder about some things pertaining to this subject, we can be confident that the Lord has given us all that we need to know in His Word. In this chapter we will allow the Bible to answer six questions commonly asked about the Second Coming of Christ.

Question #1: CAN WE BE CERTAIN THAT JESUS IS COMING AGAIN?

Jesus Said That He Would Come Again

Can we be certain that Jesus is coming again? Yes, absolutely we can be sure that He is coming again because He promised that He would. He declared: *"Let not your heart be troubled; you believe in God, believe also in Me. In My Father's house are many mansions; if it were not so, I would have told you. I go to prepare a place for you. And if I go to prepare a place for you, I will come again and receive you to Myself; that where I am, there you may be also"* (John 14:1-3 NKJV).

The Angels Said That He Would Come Again

Not only did Jesus say that He was coming again, but also the Angels said that He would come again. At the ascension of the Lord, the apostles were looking up toward heaven when two men in white apparel, no doubt angels, said to them: *"Men of Galilee, why do you stand gazing up into heaven? This same Jesus, who was taken up from you into heaven, will so come in like manner as you saw Him go into heaven"* (Acts 1:11).

The Apostles Said That He Would Come Again

In addition to the promise of Jesus, the apostles also said that Jesus would come again. Paul wrote of the Second Coming of Jesus. *"For the Lord Himself will descend from heaven..."* (I Thessalonians 4:16), and *"When the Lord Jesus is revealed from heaven with His mighty angels...when He comes in that day"* (2 Thessalonians 1:7,10). Peter wrote, *"But the day of the Lord will come as a thief in the night"* (2 Peter 3:10).

The Hebrew writer stated emphatically that the Lord would come again: *"So Christ was offered once to bear the sins of many. To those who eagerly wait for Him He will appear a second time, apart from sin, for salvation"* (Hebrews 9:28).

Among those who claim to believe the Bible, there is little disagreement that the Lord is coming again. Most differences arise as a result of speculation about the time of His coming and the purpose for which He is coming. Rather than getting caught up with the numberless opinions that have been advanced in those areas we should draw our conclusions based only on what the Bible has to say.

Question #2: WHEN IS JESUS COMING AGAIN?

No one knows when the Lord is coming again. This is something that God has reserved for Himself alone. Concerning the exact time of his second coming, Jesus said: *"But of that day and hour no one knows, not even the angels in heaven, nor the Son, but only the Father"* (Mark 13:32). God has not chosen to reveal that time to any man, but He has given us information about that coming.

Life Will Be Normal

Jesus will come at a time when life is going on as normal, just as in the days before the flood. *"But as the days of Noah were, so also will the coming of the Son of Man be. For as in the days before the flood, they were eating and drinking, marrying and giving in marriage, until the day that Noah entered the ark, and did not know until the flood came and took them all away, so also will the coming of the Son of Man be"* (Matthew 24:37-39).

His Coming Will Be Unexpected

It will be even as when a thief comes. *"But the day of the Lord will come as a thief in the night..."* (2 Peter 3:10). Since no one knows when that day will come, we are admonished to be ready. *"Therefore you also be ready, for the Son of Man is coming at an hour you do not expect"* (Matthew 24:44).

Question #3: WHAT ABOUT THOSE WHO CLAIM TO KNOW THE DAY OF HIS COMING?

Since God has not chosen to reveal that day to any man, we must conclude that those who claim to know that time are false prophets.

There have been many in the past that publicly set dates as to when the world would come to an end and Christ would come again.

One such religious leader was William Miller. He first set the date at March 21, 1844. Many honest and sincere people were deceived and waited expectantly for the Lord to come on that date. However, that day came and went, but of course the Lord did not come. Miller re-checked his figures and decided he had missed the date by seven months. He said the correct date should have been October 22, 1844. He enlisted some 700 preachers who helped him spread the message to the people to prepare for the Lord's coming on that date. As the day approached, people were filled with fear, panic, excitement, and enthusiasm. Some people even committed suicide. Those who believed Miller disposed of their personal goods, their businesses and their homes. They made themselves white robes in which they could ascend, and then waited for the Lord's appearance. October 22, 1844 came and went, but of course, the Lord did not come. [1]

William Miller is typical of many would-be prophets who have tried and failed to predict the exact time of Christ's Second Coming. All such efforts are just foolish speculation. There is not a man on the face of the earth who knows anything about the exact time when Christ will come again. That information is to be found only in the mind of God. *"But of that day and hour no one knows, not even the angels in heaven, nor the Son, but only the Father"* (Mark 13:32).

Question #4: HOW WILL HE COME AGAIN?

After failing in their prediction of Christ's second coming, some date-setters tried to cover up their mistake by saying that Christ really did come but no one saw Him. This theory is quite ridiculous in light of what the Bible says about the manner of Christ's coming. Notice what the Bible says:

First, the Bible Says That "Every Eye Will See Him"

When Jesus comes again the righteous as well as the unrighteous will see Him. The idea that the Lord will come secretly or invisibly is absurd. *"Behold He is coming with the clouds, and every eye will see Him, even they who pierced Him"* (Revelation 1:7). Acts 1:9-11 tells us that Jesus was taken up in a cloud. As He was seen going, so He will be seen returning. *"This same Jesus, who was taken up from you into heaven, will so come in like manner as you saw Him go into heaven."*

Second, We Will Hear Him Coming

Not only will we see Jesus coming, but we will hear Him as well. *"For the Lord Himself will descend from heaven with a shout, with the voice of an archangel, and with the trumpet of God. And the dead in Christ will rise first"* (I Thessalonians 4:16).

Third, He Will Come without Announcement

No warning will be given when the Lord comes again. *"For you yourselves know perfectly that the day of the Lord so comes as a thief in the night. For when they say, 'Peace and safety!' then sudden destruction comes upon them, as labor pains upon a pregnant woman. And they shall not escape"* (I Thessalonians 5:2-3).

Fourth, He Will Come on the Clouds

When Jesus was being tried, he said to the high priest: *"It is as you said. Nevertheless, I say to you, hereafter you will see the Son of Man sitting at the right hand of the Power, and coming on the clouds of heaven"* (Matt. 26:64).

Fifth, He Is Coming in Person

The Lord will come in person and we will be caught up to be with Him. *"For the Lord Himself will descend from heaven... Then we who are alive and remain shall be caught up together with them in the clouds to meet the Lord in the air"* (I Thessalonians 4:16-17).

Sixth, He Is Coming with the Angels

It will be a breathtaking scene when the Lord descends from heaven with untold numbers of angels descending with Him. *"For the Son of Man will come in the glory of His Father with His angels, and then He will reward each according to his works"* (Matt. 16:27). *"When the Son of Man comes in His glory, and all the holy angels with Him, then He will sit on the throne of His glory"* (Matthew 25:27).

Seventh, He Is Coming in Flaming Fire

Fire will accompany the second coming of the Lord: *"And to give you who are troubled rest with us when the Lord Jesus is revealed from heaven with His mighty angels, in flaming fire, taking vengeance on those who do not know God, and on those who do not obey the gospel of our Lord Jesus Christ"* (2 Thessalonians 1:7-9).

Eighth, We Will Meet Him in the Air

While there has been much speculation about the Lord's Second Coming, one very important fact is often overlooked. The Scriptures do not say that Christ will ever set foot on the earth again. On the contrary I Thessalonians. 4:17 tells us: *"Then we who are alive and remain shall be caught up together with them in the clouds to meet the Lord in the air. And thus we shall always be with the Lord."*

Question #5: WHY IS JESUS COMING AGAIN?

Perhaps we can best answer the question *"Why is He coming again?"* by first noticing why He is NOT coming.

He Is Not Coming to Set Up An Earthly Kingdom

No, contrary to what many teach, He is not coming to establish an earthly kingdom. Why? Because the Lord's kingdom has already been established. In Mark 9:1 Jesus stated that the kingdom would come during the lifetime of those who were listening to Him speak. *"Assuredly, I say to you that there are some standing here who will not taste death till they see the kingdom of God present with power."* If the kingdom has not yet been established, as some maintain, then some that were standing there with Jesus almost 2,000 years ago are still alive today! Even to suggest such a possibility is absurd.

The Kingdom Was "at Hand"

Prior to the day of Pentecost *The Kingdom was spoken of as being in the future. "The time is fulfilled, and the kingdom of God is at hand, repent, and believe in the gospel"* (Mark 1:15). *"At hand"* means it is eminent; it is coming soon. The terms *"church"* and *"kingdom"* were used interchangeably by Jesus as He responded to Peter's confession that Jesus was the Christ, the Son of God. *"And I also say to you that you are Peter, and on this rock I will build My church, and the gates of Hades shall not prevail against it. And I will give you the keys of the kingdom of heaven and whatever you bind on earth will be bound in heaven, and whatever you loose on earth will be loosed in heaven"* (Matthew 16:18-19).

The Kingdom Was Already Established

The Lord is not coming again to establish His kingdom because it has already been established; the kingdom or church came into existence on the day of Pentecost as recorded in Acts 2. The kingdom was to come with power (Mark 9:1); the power was to come with the Holy Spirit (Acts 1:8); therefore, the kingdom would come with the arrival of the Holy Spirit; the Holy Spirit came on the day of Pentecost (some fifty days after the death of Christ) and filled the apostles, enabling them to speak as the Spirit gave them utterance (Acts 2:4). The kingdom was established at that time.

The Keys of the Kingdom

Further evidence that the kingdom was established on Pentecost is the fact that the keys of the kingdom that were promised to Peter in Matthew 16:19 were used by Peter as he stood up with the eleven on the day of Pentecost. He declared the good news about Jesus and presented the means by which that great audience, as well as all the obedient as long as time should last, could have their sins forgiven.

Those who responded to the gospel message repented and were baptized (Acts 2:38), and they were added to the kingdom, the church (Acts 2:47).

The Kingdom Was Spoken of as Being in Existence

After the day of Pentecost, the kingdom (church) was spoken of as being in existence. *"And the Lord added to the church daily those who were being saved"* (Acts 2:47). Later, Acts 8:12 tells us that Philip was preaching the kingdom and baptizing. *"But when they believed Philip as he preached the things concerning the kingdom of God and the name of Jesus Christ, both men and women were baptized."* They became members of the kingdom in the same way, as did the 3000 on Pentecost.

Christians Were Already In the Kingdom

When Paul wrote to the church at Colosse he was writing to people who were already in the kingdom. He reminded the Christians there that they had been delivered from the power of darkness and conveyed *"Into the kingdom of the Son of his love"* (Colossians 1:13). There should be no question that the kingdom had to be in existence in order for the Colossians to be placed in it. No, Jesus is not coming to establish the kingdom. It has now been in existence for almost 2,000 years.

The Lord's Kingdom Is NOT of This World

That is exactly what Jesus taught in John 18:36, *"My Kingdom is not of this world."* Could the Lord have stated it any plainer? *"Now why do the premillennial advocates keep insisting that the kingdom of God is yet future, that it is not the church, and* that it is separate from the kingdom of heaven? Because they cling to their preconceived notion that the kingdom must be physical and include fleshly Israel... they want an earthly, physical kingdom and they intend to have it. *They willingly twist the Scriptures to get their way!*" [2] The kingdom came into existence in the first century, but it was not a physical, earthly kingdom as premillennialism expects.

It Is NOT an Earthly Kingdom

Jesus told the Pharisees that His kingdom was not the kind of early kingdom they apparently had in mind, *"Now when He was asked by the Pharisees when the kingdom of God would come, He answered them and said, 'The kingdom of God does not come with observation; nor will they say, See here! Or See there! For indeed the kingdom of God is within you'"* (Luke 17:20,21). He spoke of the nature of His kingdom even more clearly in John 18:36: Jesus said, *"My kingdom is not of this world. If My kingdom were of this world, My servants would fight, so that I should not be delivered to the Jews; but now My kingdom is not from here"* (John 18:36).

The means of entrance into Christ's kingdom clearly shows that it is not an earthly kingdom. It is a spiritual kingdom, and being a spiritual kingdom, it takes a spiritual birth to get into it. Again Jesus said, *"Most assuredly, I say to you, unless one is born of water and the Spirit, he cannot enter the kingdom of God"* (John 3:5). *" When you put it all together, it is not a physical kingdom at all. It is the reign of God in the heart of the believer through the truth. So, Premillennialism is all wrong on the kingdom."* [3] Most assuredly, Jesus is not coming to establish a kingdom which He already established in the first century. What else is He not coming back to do?

Jesus Is NOT Coming Back to Reign 1000 Years on Earth

Even though Jesus declared: *"My kingdom is not of this world"* (John 18:36), and refused to be made an earthly king (Matthew 6:15), there are those who insist that Jesus will come back to earth and set up a literal kingdom in Jerusalem and there reign as king with all the righteous for a thousand years. This doctrine is called premillennialism (from Latin pre before, mille a thousand, and annus a year). It should be clearly understood by the reader that there is no passage of Scripture in the entire Bible that speaks of Christ reigning over an earthly kingdom for a thousand years, either before or after His Second Coming. This is a theory based on a false interpretation of the figurative language of Revelation 20. Let's notice Revelation 20:1-6:

Revelation 20:1-6

"Then I saw an angel coming down from heaven, having the key to the bottomless pit and a great chain in his hand. He laid hold of the dragon, that serpent of old, who is the Devil and Satan, and bound him for a thousand years; and he cast him into the bottomless pit, and shut him up, and set a seal on him, so that he should deceive the nations no more till the thousand years were finished. But after these things he must be released for a little while. And I saw thrones, and they sat on them, and judgment was committed to them. Then I saw the souls of those who had been beheaded for their witness to Jesus and for the word of God, who had not worshiped the beast or his image, and had not received his mark on their foreheads or on their hands. And they lived and reigned with

Christ for a thousand years. But the rest of the dead did not live again until the thousand years were finished. This is the first resurrection. Blessed and holy is he who has part in the first resurrection. Over such the second death has no power; but they shall be priests of God and of Christ, and shall reign with Him a thousand years."

Figurative Language

The book of Revelation is a highly figurative book that is filled with symbolism. *"An examination of these first half-dozen verses of Revelation 20 reveals the following symbols: a key, a chain, a dragon or serpent, an abyss, a thousand years, thrones, a beast, marks on foreheads and hands, and a resurrection. It is certainly a strange interpretation, which contends that a figurative serpent was bound with a figurative chain and thrown into a figurative abyss, which was locked with a figurative key, to be confined for a literal thousand years. It ought to be manifestly obvious that no literal reign of Christ upon the earth is here alluded to. Even if one does not understand the specific design of the symbols, he can see the symbolic import of the thousand years."* [4]

The twentieth chapter of Revelation is the only place in the Bible that mentions a thousand-year reign, and it is done so in the midst of figures and symbols. This symbolic chapter must be made to harmonize with the plain, literal statements of the rest of the New Testament concerning the Second Coming of Christ.

A primary rule of Bible study is to never interpret symbolic language so that it conflicts with literal language. Those who promote the *"thousand-year reign"* theory violate this principle. Even though Revelation chapter 20 has been made the proof-text for those who promote the thousand-year-reign theory, please notice 6 things that this chapter does not say:

1. First, it says nothing about the Second Coming of Christ. The very foundation for the premillennialists is dependent upon the subject of the Second Coming of Jesus being in this chapter, and it is not there! It is not even suggested!

2. Second, it says nothing about the establishment of a kingdom, and certainly nothing about a literal throne of David.

3. Third, there is no mention of Jews or Gentiles reigning with Christ on earth for a thousand years. In the text the reigning ones are the martyrs, "the souls of those who had been beheaded for their witness to Jesus..." (v. 4).

4. Fourth, the text does not say that any reigning will take place on the earth. We must remember that Christ clearly stated that His kingdom was not an earthly one: "My kingdom is not of this world..." (John 18:36).

5. Fifth, there is no mention of a bodily resurrection. In his vision John saw souls, not bodies. Not one word is said about a bodily resurrection.

6. Sixth, there is no mention about Christ being on the earth.

7. All of these items are vitally important to those who hold the premillennial position, and yet, these things are all missing from the passage that they hold to be their proof-text.

Before Jesus left the earth He made this promise to His disciples: *"In My Father's house are many mansions; if it were not so I would have told you. I go to prepare a place for you. And if I go and prepare a place for you, I will come again and receive you to Myself; that where I am, there you may be also"* (John 14:2-3).

Jesus said He was going to the Father, but He would return to get the faithful and take them to that heavenly realm. There is absolutely no place in the sequence of events for a thousand-year reign of Christ in Jerusalem.

We have seen why He is NOT COMING back, now let's see why **Jesus IS coming back.**

He Is Coming Back to Raise the Dead

When Jesus comes again both sinners and Christians will be raised: *"Do not marvel at this; for the hour is coming in which all who are in the graves will hear His voice and come forth— those who have done good to the resurrection of life, and those who have done evil unto the resurrection of condemnation"* (John 5:28-29).

There is not the slightest suggestion, as some have taught, that there will be two resurrections, one for the righteous and one for sinners with one thousand years between. There will be only one resurrection. I Thessalonians 4:16 says *"And the dead in Christ will rise first,"* but the very next verse tells us to what this time sequence refers. The dead in Christ will rise and *"Then we who are alive and remain shall be caught up together with them in the clouds to meet the Lord in the air. And thus we shall always be with the Lord"* (verse 17). Paul is not talking about two resurrections;

he is showing that the living Christians will have no advantage over those who have died. The dead in Christ will be resurrected before the living saints are transformed (I Corinthians 15:51-52).

He Is Coming Back to Judge the World

Jesus declared: "*When the Son of Man comes in His glory, and all the holy angels with Him, then He will sit on the throne of His glory. All the nations will be gathered before Him, and He will separate them one from another, as a shepherd divides his sheep from the goats. And He will set the sheep on His right hand, but the goats on the left... Then He will also say to those on the left hand, 'Depart from Me, you cursed, into everlasting fire prepared for the devil and his angels'*" (Matt. 25 31-33, 41). This is a universal judgment of all nations, of the wicked and the righteous.

On the appointed day the entire world will be judged: "*Because He has appointed a day on which He will judge the world in righteousness by the Man whom He has ordained*" (Acts 17:31). All people will stand before the judgment seat of the Lord: "*For we shall all stand before the judgment seat of Christ. For it is written 'As I live, says the Lord, every knee shall bow to Me, and every tongue shall confess to God.' So then each of us shall give account of himself to God*" (Romans 14:10-12). The judging of the righteous and the wicked will take place at the same judgment. The Scriptures place the end of the world, the resurrection, and the final judgment all at the time of Christ's Second Coming. "*I charge you therefore before God and the Lord Jesus Christ, who will judge the living and the dead at His appearing and His kingdom*" (2 Tim. 4:1).

He Is Coming Back to Deliver the Kingdom to God.

The kingdom is now in existence and Christ is reigning as king. He will continue to reign until death is destroyed. That will occur when Jesus comes again and raises all the dead. *"Then comes the end, when He delivers the kingdom to God the Father, when He puts an end to all rule and all authority and power. For He must reign till He has put all enemies under His feet. The last enemy that will be destroyed is death"* (I Corinthians 15:24-26). When the last enemy, death, is destroyed, the kingdom will be delivered up to the Father and time will be no more.

Question #6: WHEN JESUS COMES AGAIN, WILL THAT BE THE END OF THE WORLD?

Yes, the end of the world will occur at the Second Coming of Jesus. This is made clear in 2 Peter 3:10-11: *"But the day of the Lord will come as a thief in the night, in which the heavens will pass away with a great noise, and the elements will melt with fervent heat; both the earth and the works that are in it will be burned up. Therefore, since all these things will be dissolved, what manner of persons ought you to be in holy conduct and godliness."*

This will mark the end of time: *"Who will confirm you to the end, that you may be blameless in the day of our Lord Jesus Christ"* (I Corinthians 1:8). In I Corinthians 15:23 Paul speaks of the *"coming"* of Christ and in the very next verse says: *"Then comes the end..."* (v. 24). When Jesus comes again the world will be no more, and time will cease to exist.

Footnotes

1. V. E. Howard, The Second Coming of Christ and the Millennium, Central Printers and Pub., W. Monroe, LA, pp. 5,6
2. Charles Cook, Millennium Mania, Star Bible and Tract Corp., Ft. Worth, TX, p. 35
3. Jerry Moffitt, Denominational Doctrines, Published by author, Portland, TX, p. 310
4. Wayne Jackson, Premillennialism, A Study of Infidelity Published by author, Stockton, CA p. 18

CHAPTER 18
WHAT IS THE "RAPTURE"?

How Does the Rapture Doctrine Fit In With the Second Coming of Christ?

The answer to that question is, the "Rapture" doesn't fit in at all. Many are surprised to learn that the "Rapture" is not a Biblical subject. The Scriptures say nothing about it. It is a concept that has been around for some time, but was highly promoted by Hal Lindsey in his book, The Late Great Planet Earth, first published in 1970.

1. According to the proponents of the theory, at the end of the "church age" Jesus will raise the righteous dead and take them, along with the righteous who are living, to a special place, presumably like heaven, for seven years where they will be given rewards and positions.

2. They teach that those people who remain on the earth will not know where the saints have gone. They will realize they are gone, but will not be able to explain their disappearance.

3. They will see the open graves that have been abandoned by the resurrected bodies, but they will have no explanation.

4. Supposedly, while this "Rapture" is going on in heaven for seven years, the "great tribulation" takes place on the earth.

5. This is to happen primarily during the last three and one-half years of the seven-year period.

6. During that time there will be fear, anxiety, and death on a massive scale.

7. Furthermore, those who advocate the "Rapture" teach that at the end of the seven-year period the righteous will go to Jerusalem with Christ and reign with Him for a thousand years.

8. Then, at the end of the thousand-year reign the wicked will be resurrected and condemned to eternal punishment.

What is Wrong with the Doctrine of the "Rapture"?

There is a great deal wrong with the man-made doctrine of the "Rapture." Although it may not be a complete list, the following includes nineteen things that make the doctrine unacceptable to the Bible believer:

1. There is no Bible basis for the "Rapture" doctrine. Will there ever be such a thing as the "Rapture"? Absolutely not! Is there a conflict between "Rapture" teaching and the plain teaching of the Bible? Absolutely!

2. The "Rapture" requires too many comings of Jesus. They have Him coming the first time to take the righteous away

for seven years. Then they have Him coming again seven years later to go to Jerusalem to reign a thousand years. Then at the end of the thousand years they have Him raising the wicked and judging them. Jude 14,15 pictures Jesus coming to execute judgment on the ungodly. So, according to the "Rapture" proponents, another coming of the Lord is required for judgment upon the wicked.

3. The Bible says that when Jesus comes He will execute judgment "upon all," not some now and some later, but all at one time. His coming will not be in stages with years between the comings. *"Behold, the Lord comes with ten thousands of His saints, to execute judgment on all, to convict all who are ungodly among them of all their ungodly deeds which they have committed in an ungodly way, and of all the harsh things which ungodly sinners have spoken against Him"* (Jude 14,15).

4. The proponents of the "Rapture" say that only a part of humanity will see Jesus when He comes the second time. Only the righteous dead and the righteous living will see Him. The remainder of those who are living will not see Him for at least seven years.

5. They say that those among the unrighteous dead will not see Him until the thousand-year reign is finished. This cannot possibly be correct because Revelation 1:7 states that when Jesus comes *"every eye will see Him, even they who pierced Him. And all the tribes of the earth will mourn because of Him."*

6. The "Rapture" is in conflict with Matthew 25:31-46. Unlike the "Rapture" theory, Matthew 25 has *"all the nations,"* the wicked as well as the good, being judged at the same time in the same judgment.

7. The "Rapture" has some of the dead being raised while others are left in the grave. However, the Bible says that Jesus will come to judge all the living and dead, the wicked and the good, all in the same judgment. There will be a great separation. The wicked are placed on the left and the righteous on the right. Those on the left will be sentenced to punishment in hell, while those on the right will get to enjoy the bliss of heaven. There is no room in Matthew 25 for a "Rapture" period, or the "great tribulation," or the thousand years between the resurrection of the righteous and the wicked.

8. Paul states in 2 Timothy 4:1, *"I charge you therefore before God and the Lord Jesus Christ, who will judge, the living and the dead at His appearing and His kingdom."* Paul said that Jesus will judge those who are living and those who are dead at His coming. Matthew 25:31-46 tells us that the judgment will contain both the righteous and the wicked. Therefore, all the wicked who are dead as well as those who are living will be judged.

9. At the same time, all the righteous who are living as well as those who are dead will be judged. In contrast, the "Rapture" has Jesus coming with no universal judgment, with only part of the dead being raised, while others are left in their graves.

10. The "Rapture" theory is in contradiction to the clear and positive teaching of the Lord in John 5:28-29. *"Do not marvel at this; for the hour is coming in which all who are in the graves will hear His voice and come forth, those who have done good to the resurrection of life, and those who have done evil, to the resurrection of condemnation."* While the "Rapture" has multiple judgments, the Bible says that all humanity will be judged at the same time, the good as well as the wicked.

11. The "Rapture" does not fit the Bible teaching of the "last day." *"This is the will of the Father who sent Me, that of all He has given Me I should lose nothing, but should raise it up as the last day. And this is the will of Him who sent Me, that of all He has given Me I should lose nothing, but should raise it up at the last day. And this is the will of Him who sent Me, that every one who sees the Son and believes in Him may have everlasting life; and I will raise him up at the last day."* ... *"No one can come to Me unless the Father who sent Me draws him; and will raise him up at the last day"* (John 6:39,40,44). *"Whoever eats My flesh and drinks My blood has eternal life, and I will raise him up at the last day"* (John 6:54). *"He who rejects Me, and does not receive My words, has that which judges him – the word that I have spoken will judge him in the last day"* (John 12:48). Jesus taught in John 5:28-29 that the resurrection of both the good and evil will take place in the same hour. That resurrection and judgment will take place in the last day. The "Rapture" theory has not just days but a thousand

years separating the resurrection and judgment of the good and evil.

12. The "Rapture" is in conflict with 2 Thessalonians 1:6-10. *"Since it is a righteous thing with God to repay with tribulation those who trouble you, and to give you who are troubled rest with us when the Lord Jesus is revealed from heaven with His mighty angels, in flaming fire taking vengeance on those who do not know God, and on those who do not obey the gospel of our Lord Jesus Christ. These shall be punished with everlasting destruction from the presence of the Lord and from the glory of His power, when He comes, in that Day, to be glorified in His saints and to be admired among all those who believe, because our testimony among you was believed."* In this passage Paul spoke of two groups. The first group is composed of those who have been troubled and persecuted. These are the obedient. The other group is described as those who do not know God and have not obeyed the gospel.

13. In 2 Thessalonians 1:6-10 He also talks about two compensations. To the afflicted He will give rest, but to the disobedient He will bring punishment. The rest for the righteous and punishment for the disobedient will occur in "that day" when Jesus comes with His angels.

14. The "Rapture" does not have the wicked receiving their punishment in "that day" as Paul declared, but a thousand years later!

15. According to the "Rapture" doctrine, the righteous will be in the air and the wicked will still be on the earth.

16. The "Rapture" conflicts with 2 Peter 3:10-14. *"But the day of the Lord will come as a thief in the night, in which the heavens will pass away with a great noise, and the elements will melt with fervent heat; but the earth and the elements will pass away with a great noise; both the earth and the works that are in it will be burned up. Therefore, since all these things will be dissolved, what manner of persons ought you to be in holy conduct and godliness, looking for and hastening the coming of the day of God, because of which the heavens will be dissolved, being on fire, and the elements will melt with fervent heat? Nevertheless we, according to His promise, look for new heavens and a new earth in which righteousness dwells. Therefore, beloved, looking forward to these things, be diligent to be found by Him in peace, without spot and blameless."* This passage refers to the Second Coming of Jesus. When that happens, the earth and all in it will be burned up.

17. But, the "Rapture" demands a continuation of the earth after the Lord comes. They say the earth will continue seven more years until Jesus returns to Jerusalem, and then a thousand more years after that.

18. Those who advocate the doctrine of the "Rapture" teach that the earth will be renovated to be the resting-place for those who are not among the fortunate 144,000 who will be in heaven. Compare this far-fetched theory with the Bible

that clearly says the earth and all in it will be burned up at the Lord's Second Coming.

19. There are two primary passages that the advocates for the "Rapture" use in an attempt to support this imaginative theory. Neither the word "Rapture" nor the teaching to verify it is to be found in either one. They both refer to the Second Coming of Christ with no reference whatsoever to a "Rapture."

The first passage "Rapture" advocates use to support their theory is I Thessalonians 4:13-17. One does not have to look very long to realize that this passage in no way verifies the "Rapture." The proponents of the "Rapture" say that Jesus will come in secret, but this passage tells us that when Jesus comes it will not be in secret. *"He will descend with a shout, with the voice of the archangel, and with the trump of God"* (v. 16). The coming of Christ mentioned in this passage is the same as the one mentioned in Revelation 1:7. *"Behold, He is coming with clouds, and every eye will see Him, even they who pierced Him."* There is no secret coming discussed here. These Scriptures say that there will be a shout, the voice of the archangel, the trump of God, and every eye seeing Jesus when He comes again.

The second passage that the advocates of the "Rapture" use is I Corinthians 15:50-58. It is equally lacking in support for the theory. Verse 52 dispels the idea of a secret coming when it tells us that the sound of a trumpet will accompany the Lord. There is more in this passage that does not fit the "Rapture." When Jesus comes, immortality will begin (v. 53). Death will be destroyed at His coming, *"swallowed up in victory"* (v. 54). In contrast, "Rapture" proponents say that life and death will continue on earth during the time the righteous are with Jesus. These passages do not verify the "Rapture," but in fact, they repudiate this false doctrine.

Is the Church a Substitute for the Kingdom?

Premillennialism traditionally has considered the church to be an afterthought in God's plan, a stop-gap, emergency arrangement, necessitated by the failure of the Jews to accept Christ when He came to establish His kingdom among them as planned. "With His purpose thwarted by the unreceptive Jews, His time-table of the Seventy Weeks (Dan. 9) disrupted, and a resurrected Christ on His hands with nothing to do, God hastily designed the church as a receptacle for that handful of disciples who did respond to the kingdom call, and diverted the thrust of His attention to the Gentile world until He should see fit to make another try at reaching the obdurate Jews." 2

"Premillennialism implies that the death of Christ was an unscheduled contingency, the culmination of that Jewish rejection which thwarted God's plan for Christ's first advent. Had the Jews accepted their king, presumably He would not have died. Premillennialists are not, of course, specific about this, but so it would seem." 3

The Bible is clear that the death of Christ and the establishment of His kingdom, the church, were in the plan of God from the beginning. Acts 2:23 leaves no room for doubt: *"Him, being delivered by the determined purpose and foreknowledge of God, you have taken by lawless hands, have crucified, and put to death."* The death of Christ was no accident. It was prophesied in the Old Testament that Christ would be rejected and would be killed. *"He was despised and rejected of men"* (Isaiah 53:3). *"He was cut off out of the land of the living"* (Isaiah 53:8).

Christ knew His purpose was to die during the earliest days of His personal ministry, before the opposition of the Jews developed against Him: *"And I, if I am lifted up from the earth, will draw all peoples to Myself. This He said, signifying by what death He would die"* (John 12:32-33). *"From that time Jesus began to show to His disciples that He must go to Jerusalem, and suffer many things from the elders and chief priests and scribes, and be killed, and be raised the third day"* (Matt. 16:21).

Jesus looked upon His death as a fulfillment of His purpose. *"Now my soul is troubled, and what shall I say? 'Father, save Me from this hour'? But for this purpose I came to this hour"* (John 12:27).

The Church Was Planned by God

The death of Christ and the establishment of the church were in the mind of God from the beginning. Well in advance of His crucifixion Jesus stated His intention to build His church. *"And I also say to you that you are Peter, and on this rock I will build My church, and the gates of Hades shall not prevail against it"* (Matt. 16:18).

The church was no afterthought. It was planned, promised, and then built. So precious was the church to God that He had His own Son die in order to purchase it. *"...Shepherd the church of God which He purchased with His own blood"* (Acts 20:28). *"...Just as Christ also loved the church and gave Himself for her"* (Ephesians 5:25). The church was no afterthought. It was in the eternal purpose of God that the church would declare the wisdom of God to the world. *"To the intent that now the manifold wisdom of God might be made known by the church to the principalities and powers in the heavenly places, according to the eternal purpose which He accomplished in Christ Jesus our Lord"* (Ephesians 3:10-11). How much clearer could the Scriptures have been in telling us that the church was planned from the beginning?

Conclusion

The Second Coming of Jesus and the judgment should be sobering thoughts to all of us. The "Rapture" should have no part in our thinking. At the judgment each one will hear God's final sentence, eternal bliss in heaven or eternal judgment in hell. The warning to be prepared for that time cannot be over emphasized. Preparation must be now.

When we hear the Lord coming it will be too late to begin that preparation. By God's grace He has made it possible for every man to have his sins forgiven through the blood that Jesus shed on the cross.

1. "For by grace you have been saved through faith..." (Ephesians 2:8).
2. "He who believes and is baptized will be saved..." (Mark 16:16).
3. "Repent, and let every one of you be baptized in the name of Jesus Christ for the remission of sins..." (Acts 2:38).

When one applies the blood of Jesus to his soul by obedience to the gospel, his sins are removed and will not be held against him at the judgment: *"Their sins and their lawless deeds I will remember no more"* (Hebrews 8:12).

There's a great day coming,
A great day coming,

There's a great day coming by and by;
When the saints and the sinners
Shall be parted right and left,
Are you ready for that day to come?
-Will L. Thompson

"Therefore, you also be ready, for the Son of Man is coming at an hour you do not expect" (Matt. 24:44).

Footnotes

1. V. E. Howard, Premillennialism, Published by author, W. Monroe, LA, pp. 53-58
2. J. Curtis Manor, Denominational Doctrines, Vol. 2, Gospel Teachers Pub., Inc., Dallas, TX, p.55
3. Ibid, p. 56

CHAPTER 19
HOW CAN I SHARE THE MESSAGE OF CHRIST WITH OTHERS?

This chapter contains a suggested method for teaching others about the Lord. With this method, you use your own Bible, marking the subjects you are discussing in the margin, as well as the Scriptures that pertain to each subject. In preparation to study the Bible with others, begin by marking your Bible in the following manner. This will help you begin the study and carry the study along, providing a smooth transition as you go from passage to passage. This will eliminate the necessity of referring to a separate booklet or outline.

1. Begin on the inside cover of your Bible and write "Start– Isaiah 55:8-9."

2. Turn to that passage and write in the upper left corner, "Isaiah 55:8-9." After the citation, briefly identify the contents, such as "God's ways are not man's ways."

3. Highlight or underline those verses so that you can quickly locate the passage on the page. (Use dry markers that will not bleed through the page.)

4. At the bottom of that page in your Bible write "Next - Proverbs 14:12."

5. Turn to Proverbs 14:12 and write that citation in the upper left corner of the page, followed by the identification of the passage, "What seems right to man may not be right before God."

6. Highlight or underline that passage in your Bible.

7. At the bottom of the page write "Next - Leviticus 10:1-6."

8. Turn to Leviticus 10:1-6 and write that citation in the upper left corner of the page, followed by "Nadab and Abihu killed."

9. Highlight or underline that passage.

10. In the manner described above, continue with each passage suggested in the outline.

11. Some passages will be used more than once for different points. It is very important that you identify the subject as it is noted in the outline. In addition, use numbers to identify the order in which the passages are used. Use the same number at the bottom of the page to identify the appropriate "Next" passage. If you use "non-bleeding" colored highlighters, you can color the citation at the top of the page the same as the "Next" at the bottom of the page for a quick identification.

12. If it is comfortable for the student, let him or her read the scriptures aloud with you. As the teacher, you should study each passage in advance so that you understand its meaning. If possible, let the student draw the lesson out of each passage that is read.

13. Important: Your student may be ready for baptism before the entire study is completed. If this happens, baptize the student without delay! After the baptism, continue with the remainder of the study to help the new convert with Christian living.

Now You Are Ready to Begin the Study of Sharing the Message of Christ

1. To begin the study a short introduction such as the following would be in order. Introduction: To the student you may say, "Nothing in the world is more important than pleasing God. You are to be commended for your interest in spiritual matters and your desire to study the Bible. As we begin to study the Word, we must prepare our minds to accept the truths that are contained therein."

2. Please notice that God's thoughts and ways are different than man's thoughts and ways (Isaiah 55:8-9).

   a. What seems right to a man may be wrong in God's eyes (Proverbs 14:12).

   b. Nadab and Abihu were priests, but were killed for substituting what they wanted for what God wanted (Leviticus 10:1-6).

   c. Naaman was cleansed of leprosy, but only after he listened to God and obeyed Him (2 Kings 5:1-14).

   d. A young prophet was very sincere, but he believed a lie that was told by a religious leader and died as a result (I Kings 13:1-26).

e. The Old Testament was taken out of the way and replaced with the New Testament (Hebrews 9:15-18, Hebrews 10:9).

f. The Old Testament remains for our learning (Romans 15:4).

g. Living under the New Testament, God speaks to us through His Son (Hebrews 1:1-2).

h. God said we are to listen to Jesus (Matthew 17:1-5).

i. We will be judged by the words of Jesus (John 12:48).

j. We are told to reject any other gospel, even if it comes from an angel (Galatians 1:8-9).

k. The Word contains all about life and godliness (2 Peter 1:3).

l. Scripture is inspired by God and therefore profitable in many ways (2 Timothy 3:16-17).

m. In the parable of the soils, the seed is the Word. The soils represent the various ways people accept or reject the Word (Luke 8:5-15).

n. The Word must be handled with reverence (Revelation 22:18-19).

3. The problem of sin is universal. All have sinned and fall under sin's condemnation.

a. The one who practices sin is of the devil (I John 3:8).

b. Death comes to all men because of sin (Romans 5:12).

c. If you are outside of Christ, you personally fall under this condemnation (Romans 6:23).

d. However, those who are in Christ are not condemned as sinners (Romans 8:1-10).

e. It is by the love, mercy, and grace of God that salvation has been extended to man (Ephesians 2:4-8).

f. Jesus died so that eternal life could be offered to all men (I John 2:2).

4. How does one get into Christ where there is no condemnation?

a. By inspiration Paul taught that we get into Christ by being baptized into Him (Romans 6:3-4).

b. We are baptized into Christ and clothed with Christ (Galatians 3:26-27).

5. Baptism is the final step that puts one into Christ, but what leads up to this point? What is the full plan of salvation? What must one do to be saved?

a. Step #1 - Faith: We must believe in Jesus.
- Without faith, it is impossible to please God (Hebrews 11:6).
- Without faith in Jesus we are condemned (Mark 16:16).
- Without faith we will die in our sins (John 8:24).
- How does faith come? It comes from the Word (Romans

10:17).
- We must have the kind of faith that will cause us to obey God (John 3:36).
- Faith alone on our part is not enough to make us pleasing to God (James 2:24).

b. Step #2 - Repent: Repentance is a change of mind that brings about a change of life (Acts 26:20).
- The goodness of God leads us to repentance (Romans 2:4).
- All are commanded to repent (Acts 17:30).
- If we do not repent we will perish spiritually (Luke 13:3).
- We must repent so that our sins will be blotted out (Acts 3:19).
- God wants all to come to repentance (2 Peter 3:9).

c. Step #3 - Confess Christ: We must confess our faith in Jesus as God's Son.
- We must confess Jesus or He will deny us (Matthew 10:32-33).
- We must confess Jesus as the Son of God (I John 4:14-15).
- Before the Ethiopian eunuch was baptized, it was necessary for him to confess Christ (Acts 8:37 NKJV).
- Confession is made, leading to salvation (Romans 10:9-10).

d. Step #4 - Baptism: After we confess Jesus as God's Son, we must be baptized (immersed) in water in order to have the forgiveness of our sins.
- Jesus commanded baptism in the name of the Father, the

Son, and the Holy Spirit (Matthew 28:19).
- Jesus taught that belief, in addition to baptism results in salvation (Mark 16:16).
- Peter preached that repentance, in addition to Baptism, is for the forgiveness of sins (Acts 2:38).
- Peter commanded Cornelius and those present with him to be baptized (Acts 10:48).
- Saul was told to be baptized to wash away his sins (Acts 22:16).
- Peter said that baptism saves us (I Peter 3:21).

6. It is important that we learn what the New Testament teaches about baptism.

a. It is a burial into Christ's death and a resurrection to a new life (Romans 6:3:4).

b. We are buried with Him and raised up with Him (Colossians 2:12).

c. Baptism is in water (Acts 10:47).

d. It is a "going down" into water, and a "coming up" out of the water (Acts 8:36-38).

e. It is being born of water and the Spirit (John 3:3-5).

f. At baptism our sins are washed away (Acts 22:16).

g. We are washed with pure water (Hebrews 10:22).

h. Our sins are washed away by the blood of Jesus in baptism (Hebrews 9:22).

i. At baptism we enter the Lord's church (Acts 2:47).

j. At baptism our sins are forgiven (Acts 2:38).

k. At baptism we put on Christ and become children of God (Galatians 3:26-27).

l. At baptism we become new creatures (2 Corinthians 5:17).

m. Baptism is a command to be obeyed and not an option (Acts 10:48).

n. There is only one valid baptism (Ephesians 4:4).

7. We become Christians today in exactly the same way as those people in the New Testament did. The Book of Acts records several cases of conversion.

   a. There were 3,000 on the day of Pentecost who became Christians (Acts 2:36-42,47).

   b. Some Samaritans obeyed and became Christians (Acts 8:4-13).

   c. An Ethiopian treasurer became a Christian (Acts 8:26-40).

   d. Saul of Tarsus, later known as Paul the Apostle, became a Christian (Acts 9:1-20). Also, you may read two other accounts of this same conversion in Acts 22:3-16, and Acts 26:12-19.

    e. Cornelius and those with him in Caesarea became Christians (Acts 10:24-48, Acts 11:1-18).

    f. Lydia and her household became Christians at Philippi (Acts 16:13-15).

    g. A Jailer at Philippi and his family became Christians (Acts 16:23-24).

    h. Some Corinthians became Christians (Acts 18:8).

    i. Some disciples of John were baptized into Christ at Ephesus (Acts 19:1-7).

8. When we follow the examples of those who became Christians in New Testament times, we will become "Christians Only" as they were. We will become members of the same church of which they were members. (Acts 2:47)

Members of the church were referred to by several different terms in the Bible. These add to our understanding of the Christian's relationship to the Lord.

    a. They were called "members of the body of Christ" (I Corinthians 12:27).
    b. They were also called "disciples" (learners) of Christ (Acts 6:1,7).

    c. They were "believers in the Lord" (Acts 5:14).

d. All Christians were called "saints" (Romans 1:7).

e. All Christians were called "priests" (I Peter 2:5,9).

f. They were called "children of God" (I John 3:1-2).

g. The disciples were called "Christians" (Acts 11:26).

h. A king was almost persuaded to be a Christian (Acts 26:28).

i. "If anyone suffers, let him suffer as a Christian" (I Peter 4:16).

9. We should know that the church ....

a. Was built by Jesus (Matthew 16:18).

b. Was purchased with the blood of Jesus (Acts 20:28).

c. Was built on the foundation of Jesus (I Corinthians 3:11).

d. Was not built upon Peter or any other man (I Corinthians 1:12-13).

e. Is composed of those who have been saved (Acts 2:47).

f. Is loved by Jesus (Ephesians 5:25).

g. Has Jesus as its head (Ephesians 5:23).

h. Is the same as the "body" with Jesus as its only head

(Colossians 1:18).

i. Is singular. There is only "one body" (Ephesians 4:4). Therefore, there is only one church.

10. We should know how the church is referred to in the Bible. This will give us insight into various functions of the church. The church is:

   a. "The temple of God" (I Corinthians 3:16).

   b. The "bride" of Christ (Ephesians 5:24).

   c. The "body" of Christ (Colossians 1:18).

   d. A "kingdom" (Hebrews 12:28).

   e. The "kingdom of the Son of His love" (Colossians 1:13).

   f. The "house of God" and the "church of the Living God" (I Timothy 3:15).

   g. The "church of God" (I Corinthians 1:2).

   h. Called the "flock" (Acts 20:28).

   i. The "church of the first born" (Hebrews 12:23).

   j. Christ's church. Jesus said, "I will build my church" (Matthew 16:18).

   k. Paul used the phrase "churches of Christ" to refer

to congregations of the church (Romans 16:16).

11. We should know about the government of the church.

   a. The head of the church is Jesus. The church is His body (Ephesians 1:22-23).

   b. Each congregation selects a plurality of qualified elders for the oversight of that congregation only. The terms "elder," "bishop," and "overseer" all refer to the same office.

   c. Qualifications for elders are given in I Timothy 3:1-7.

   d. Qualifications for elders are also found in Titus 1:5-9.

   e. Some of the responsibilities of elders are found in Acts 20:28 and I Peter 5:1-4.

   f. The bishops and deacons were in the church at Philippi (Phil. 1:1).

   g. Each congregation selects deacons who are special servants for the congregation. Their qualifications are found in I Timothy 3:8-13).

   h. Preachers are selected by the local congregation to work with that congregation.
   i. They are to preach the Word, reprove, rebuke, and exhort (2 Tim. 4:1-4).

   j. They are to be good examples to the church (I Tim. 4:11-16).

k. Teachers are selected to teach the Word. "And He gave some as.... teachers" (Ephesians 4:11). We need to study to be qualified teachers (Hebrews 5:12). Teachers have a great responsibility before the Lord (James 3:1).

l. Members, including the preacher, deacons, and teachers, all work and serve under the oversight of the elders. The elders watch over their souls as those who will have to give an account to the Lord (Hebrews 13:17).

12. As Christians we need to become part of a local congregation. We will participate with other Christians as we...

    a. Faithfully attend the worship services (Hebrews 10:25).

    b. Worship in spirit and truth (John 4:23-24).

    c. Pray together:
- For one another (James 5:16).
- For all men (I Timothy 2:1-2).
- Without ceasing (I Thessalonians 5:17).
- In the name of Jesus (Ephesians 5:20).

    d. Sing together in the assembly. (There is authority only for vocal music. There is no authority for using instrumental music in worship.)
- We are to admonish one another in our singing (Colossians 3:16).
- We are to sing and make melody in our hearts (Ephesians 5:19).

e. Read Scriptures and teach (I Timothy 4:13).

   f. Observe the Lord's Supper:
   - Christ instituted it (Matthew 26:26-30).
   - We are to partake of it on the first day of the week (Acts 20:7).
   - Paul reminds us of the time when Jesus instituted the Lord's Supper and gives instructions concerning its observance (I Corinthians 11:20-30).

   g. Give liberally to support the work of the church.
   - The contribution is to be given on the first day of the week (I Corinthihans 16:1-2).
   - Macedonian congregations were poor but gave liberally (2 Corinthians. 8:1-5).
   - Will reap as we sow (2 Corinthians 9:6-8).
   - "Give and it will be given to you" (Luke 6:38).

   h. Build each other up spiritually (I Thessalonians 5:11).

   i. Do good to all men (Galatians 6:10).

13. As individual Christians we will make every effort to ...

   a. Add the Christian graces (2 Peter 1:5-11).

   b. Obey the civil government (Romans 13:1-4).

   c. Put on the whole armor of God (Ephesians 6:11-20).

   d. Bear fruit for Him (John 15:7-8).

e. Fight the good fight of faith (I Timothy 6:12).

f. Love and pray for our enemies (Matthew 5:44-48).

g. Present our bodies as living sacrifices (Romans 12:1-2).

h. Overcome evil with good (Romans 12:21).

i. Treat others as we would want to be treated (Matthew 7:12).

j. Help those in need (James 1:27).

k. Keep ourselves undefiled (James 1:27).

l. Set a good example (Titus 2:7-8).

m. Grow in grace and knowledge (2 Peter 3:18).

n. Bear the burdens of others (Galatians 6:1-2).

o. Seek the best for others (I Corinthians 10:33).

p. Seek the kingdom of God first (Matthew 6:33).

q. Demonstrate the fruit of the Spirit (Galatians 5:22-23).

r. Do the will of the Father (Matthew 7:21).

s. Glorify God in our bodies (I Corinthians 6:19-20).

t. Run the Christian race (Hebrews 12:1-2).

u. Love the brethren (I Peter 1:22).

v. Control fleshly desires (Colossians 3:5-11).

w. Seek the things above (Colossians 3:1-2).

x. Deny ungodliness and worldly desires (Titus 2:12).

y. Teach the Word to others (Acts 8:4).

z. Remain faithful to the end of our lives (Revelation 2:10).

Conclusion

The Christian life is absolutely the best life that one can live. Heaven is a certainty in the hereafter for those who give their lives to the Lord, and who faithfully live for Him (Revelation 2:10). But, even if there were no heaven in the hereafter, the Christian life would still be the best life to live. As Christians we have the "abundant life" here (John 10:10), and we can rejoice, knowing with certainty that if we live for Him faithfully, there is heaven awaiting us for our eternal dwelling place. "He who overcomes shall inherit all things, and I will be his God and he shall be My son" (Revelation 21:7).

MORE FROM V. GLENN MCCOY

RETURN TO THE OLD PATHS

Too few members of the Lord's church today are aware of the Restoration Movement and the tremendous debt that is owed to those men who called us back to the New Testament pattern. In this book we tell the story of some of the spiritual giants who suffered and sacrificed in order to preach the pure gospel and restore the church of the New Testament. We owe it to these pioneers, as well as to ourselves, to honor and cherish their memory. As we read about their labors, sufferings, and sacrifices, we may feel a little embarassed as we compare the ease of modern day preaching with that of the pioneer preachers. Much of our spiritual heritage came to us as a result of men who were willing to give their all. They did what had to be done, and their examples inspire us.

The men about whom we will study were by no means perfect. Indeed they were men with "feet of clay." They made mistakes. Many times they had to admit they were wrong and turn in a different direction. As they worked their way out of the darkness of denominationalism, they often stumbled. It is important, however, to emphasize that we do not recognize these pioneer preachers as our authorities in religion. The only authority that we are concerned about comes from the Lord by His Word. While we honor these men for their work, we do not justify our religious practices because of their teachings. If we cannot give a "thus saith the Lord," we have no business practicing it.

This 385-page softcover book by V. Glenn McCoy is designed to provide a history of the restoration movement.
Purchase at store.wvbs.org

"Thus saith the Lord, stand in the way and see, and ask for the old paths, where is the good way, and walk therein"
(Jeremiah 6:16)

Made in the USA
Columbia, SC
25 June 2022